Mathemactivit

by
Bob Bernstein

illustrated by Bron Smith

Cover by Bron Smith

Copyright © Good Apple, 1991

ISBN No. 0-86653-617-5

Printing No. 98765432

Good Apple
1204 Buchanan St., Box 299
Carthage, IL 62321-0299

S I M O N   &   S C H U S T E R   A Paramount Communications Company

Dedication

This book is dedicated to education . . . to those who cause it and to those who provide it. It is the children who are ones that will ultimately benefit from a teacher's dedication. I hope this book will make the teacher's job somewhat easier and the student's progress somewhat greater.

Table of Contents

GA1336

Introduction

The theme for *Mathemactivities* is encouraging the development of a WINNING ATTITUDE. In using the words *winning attitude*, I am not referring to winning a game or coming in first. My WINNING ATTITUDE refers to each child's positive self-esteem. It speaks about ideas that say, "I can do it! I am capable of learning, of striving to reach high expectations, . . . I can multiply and divide , . . . I AM A WINNER!"

This book offers the teacher various alternative approaches when teaching elementary mathematics. One of the main ingredients in the making of super teachers is the idea that super teachers are able to offer alternative approaches in concept presentations. This book will provide many of these approaches.

An important part of good math deals with the first five to ten minutes . . . known as the warm-up. This part of the lesson sets the tone for the remainder of the lesson. Make the warm-up interesting, exciting and creative. This will encourage your students to nourish and maintain a positive WINNING ATTITUDE. You will come across many creative warm-ups in this book. Use your gift of creativity. As you implement the pages in your daily instructions, you will see ways in which you will be able to place yourself and become a part of each activity. As you present these ideas, you may want to make them more difficult or somewhat easier depending upon the level of your youngsters. This book will offer you an idea. You take it from there. Photocopy the work pages. The ideas can be used for large or small group presentations.

Above all enjoy the book, enjoy the students and hold on to a WINNING ATTITUDE!

GA1336

You Are an Absolutely Totally Awesome and Outstanding Student!

SKILLS: Estimation
Graphing
Interpreting Data

I couldn't have said it better!

Great Statement . . . Exceptional Words

This statement can lead to some very interesting discoveries. It is made up of nine words. Rewrite each word in alphabetical order. Use the order to record the amount of times each letter is used. Record one tally for each letter.

You Are an Absolutely Totally Awesome and Outstanding Student!

Reread the statement once again. This time be ready to guess at the following:

Problem A

1. How many consonants are in the statement? _____

2. How many vowels are in the statement? _____

3. The statement contains how many syllables? _____

4. What is your guess as to the letter used most often? _____

5. The sentence is made up of fifty-three letters.

   What is the percentage of vowels? _____

   What is the percentage of consonants? _____

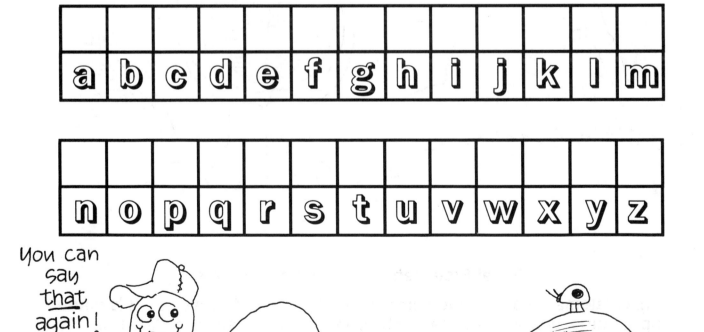

You can say that again!

2

GA1336

A Perfect 10

SKILLS: Decimals
             Averages
             Basic Computational Skills

If you were given a scale with a range of 1 to 10, 1 is at the low end of the scale and 10 is at the upper end of the scale. Considering 10 as a perfect score, how would you and your class rate certain things, events or places?

To develop some type of a rating system that will offer insights as to your classes' likes and dislikes, select a panel of eight students. Give each student a marker or crayon and some 5″ x 7″ cards. The cards should have a vertical line drawn through the middle of each. There should also be a decimal point at the bottom of the line.

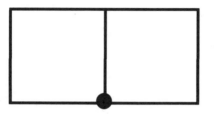

Inform all of the panel members that they will be asked to rate various things. They can do this by recording a number from 1 (low) to a perfect 10 (high). The rating can be expressed in units or units and tenths:

Suppose the class has requested that the panel members rate their like or dislike regarding blueberries.

Each panel member is to record his/her rating on the 5" x 7" card. Once the panel members have recorded their ratings, the teacher is to ask for their responses. This information is recorded at the chalkboard.

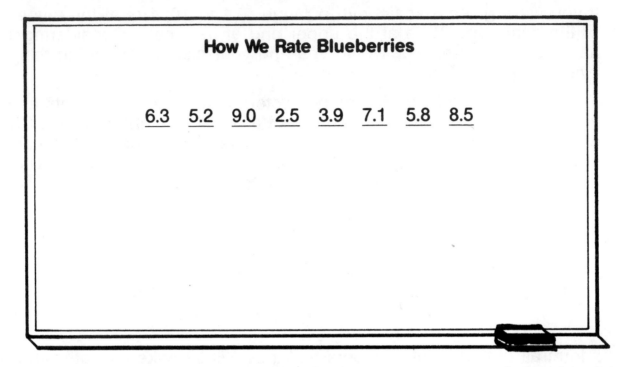

How We Rate Blueberries

6.3 5.2 9.0 2.5 3.9 7.1 5.8 8.5

The teacher will then erase the highest response and the lowest response. In this example, erase the 9.0 and the 2.5. The remaining numbers should be added. Once this sum is determined, divide this total by 6 (the six remaining responses).

6.3	6.3	6.1
5.2	5.2	6 ⟌36.8
9.0	3.9	36
2.5	7.1	8
3.9	5.8	6
7.1	8.5	2
5.8	36.8	
8.5		

The rating for blueberries is 6.1 .

What's that? a weather balloon?

Haven't you ever seen a blueberry, lady?

GA1336

Additional things you might want to rate:

1. various school subjects (math, reading, science)

2. lunch period

3. a particular book

4. various holidays

5. vacation sites

6. feelings . . . to what degree are we kind to each other?
   how much respect do we show each other?

GA1336

Change for a Dollar

SKILLS: Money
              Addition Facts
              Problem Solving

Did you know that there are many ways of making change for a dollar?
Just to name a few . . . 20 nickels
                             50 pennies and 2 quarters
                             7 dimes, 1 quarter and 5 pennies
                             how about 7 dimes, 1 quarter and 1 nickel?

When you think about it, actually there are close to 300 ways that one is able to make change of a George Washington, one dollar, United States bill.

The object of this activity is that each student in your class will be allowed to take home one, two or three blank "dollars" and with the use of colorful markers or crayons, bring these replicas to school with names for a dollar.

Every colorful response should then be mounted onto a bulletin board. It should be a bulletin board that all of the class members can marvel and take pride in. You might want to allow the activity to continue for two or three weeks.

Can be photocopied and enlarged for use as a math bulletin board.
Surround this with colorful new names for a dollar.

GA1336

Blank "dollars" to be photocopied and then cut out.

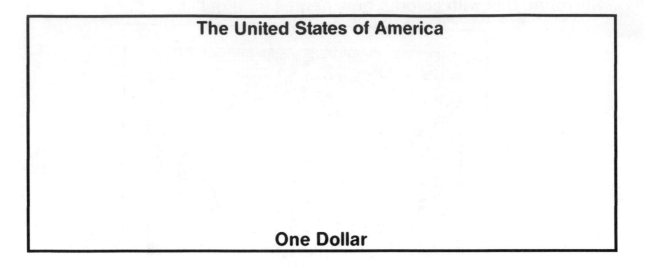

The United States of America

One Dollar

The United States of America

One Dollar

The United States of America

One Dollar

Hmm .. m . m .. Older Than I Thought

Complete each problem with a new age.

A. Scott . . . 12 years, 3 months _____	B. David . . . 11 years _____
C. Alan . . . 6 years, 7 months _____	D. Michele . . . 9 years, 8 months _____
E. Larry . . . 10 years, 4 months _____	F. Robert . . . 14 years _____
G. Amanda . . . 2 years, 11 months _____	H. Danika . . . 7 years, 7 months _____
I. Jerry . . . 11 months _____	J. Gerry . . . 1 year, 1 month _____

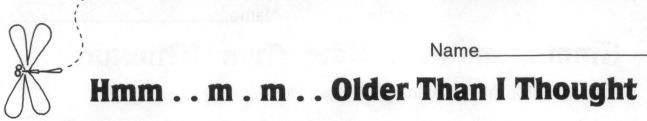

Name_____

Hmm . . m . m . . Older Than I Thought

Find the true age of each student.

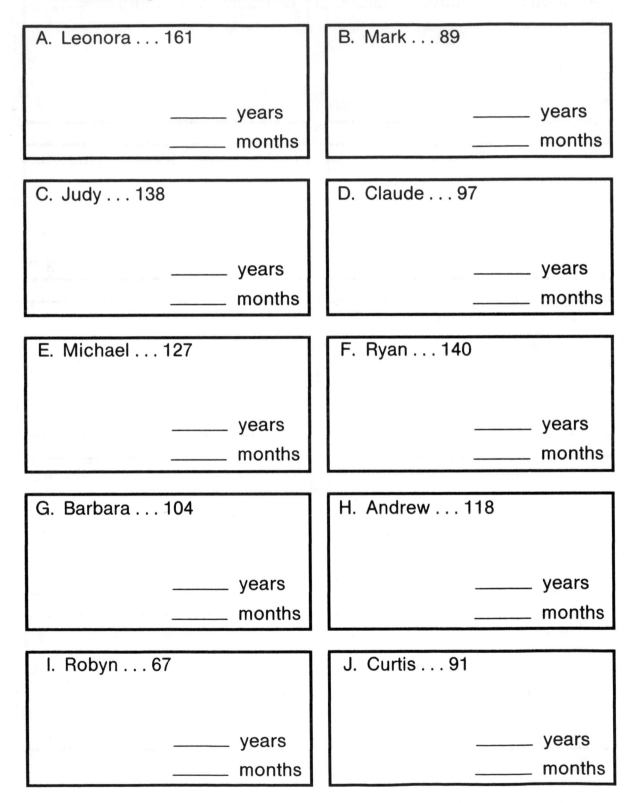

A. Leonora . . . 161

_____ years
_____ months

B. Mark . . . 89

_____ years
_____ months

C. Judy . . . 138

_____ years
_____ months

D. Claude . . . 97

_____ years
_____ months

E. Michael . . . 127

_____ years
_____ months

F. Ryan . . . 140

_____ years
_____ months

G. Barbara . . . 104

_____ years
_____ months

H. Andrew . . . 118

_____ years
_____ months

I. Robyn . . . 67

_____ years
_____ months

J. Curtis . . . 91

_____ years
_____ months

GA1336

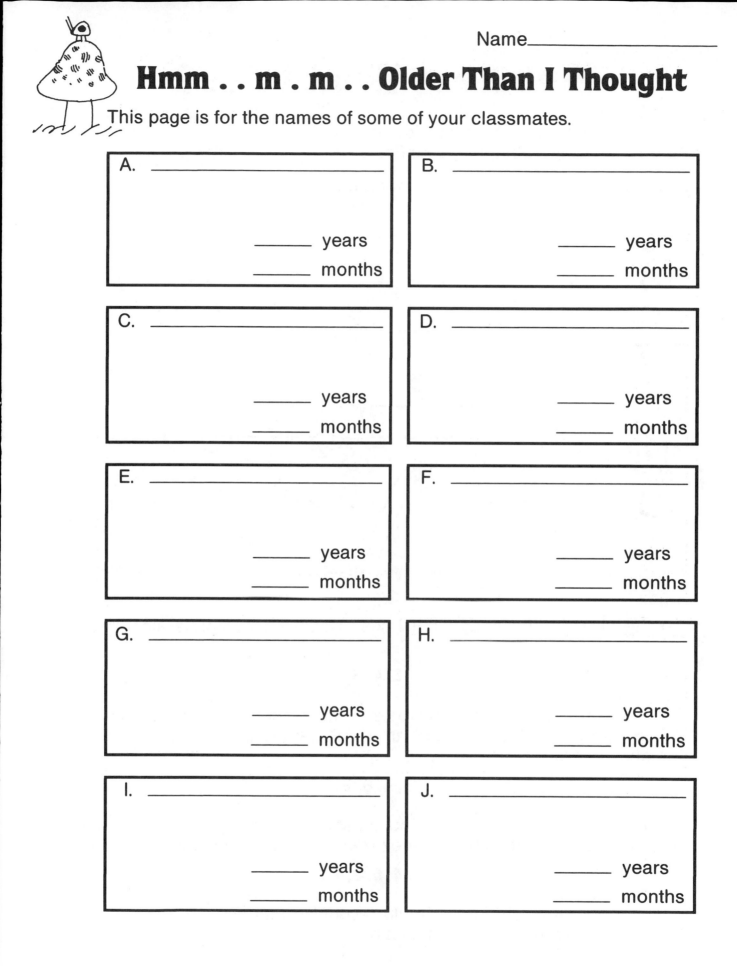

Hmm . . m . m . . Older Than I Thought

This page is for the names of some of your classmates.

A. _____

_____ years
_____ months

B. _____

_____ years
_____ months

C. _____

_____ years
_____ months

D. _____

_____ years
_____ months

E. _____

_____ years
_____ months

F. _____

_____ years
_____ months

G. _____

_____ years
_____ months

H. _____

_____ years
_____ months

I. _____

_____ years
_____ months

J. _____

_____ years
_____ months

Who Sees What I See?

SKILLS: Creative Drill for Developing
Basic Computational Facts

On the chalkboard write the following numerals:

5
4
6
8
7
10
3
9
2

Here's a new stick of chalk for you!

To the class: "Who sees what I see? Read the numerals along with me."

5, 4, 6

To get more students to participate in the response, start reading the numerals again. This time add an additional numeral from the list on the chalkboard.

5, 4, 6, 8

Once again start reading the numerals from the top of the list and emphasize, "Who sees what I see? Read the numerals along with me."

5, 4, 6, 8, 7

At this point most students should recognize that you are reading the numeral sequence on the chalkboard.

GA1336

To the class: "I would like all of you to read along with me as I read the numerals on the chalkboard, only this time I am going to make some changes to each numeral. Whatever change I make to the first numeral, I will do the same thing to all of the other numerals on the chalkboard."

"Who sees what I see? Read the numerals along with me."

6, 5, 7

again . . .

6, 5, 7, 9

once again . . . .

6, 5, 7, 9, 8

At this point, let the class know that you have added 1 to each numeral in the sequence.

A great many options are now available in attempting to develop a creative basic number facts drill. The exercise is now open-ended.

Some examples: Subtract all the numerals by 1.

Multiply all the numerals by 4.

Divide all the numerals by 2.

The class should now be ready for any number pattern you might want to drill.

21

GA1336

Who Sees What I See?

The first three answers are given in each problem. Fill in the boxes with the correct responses.

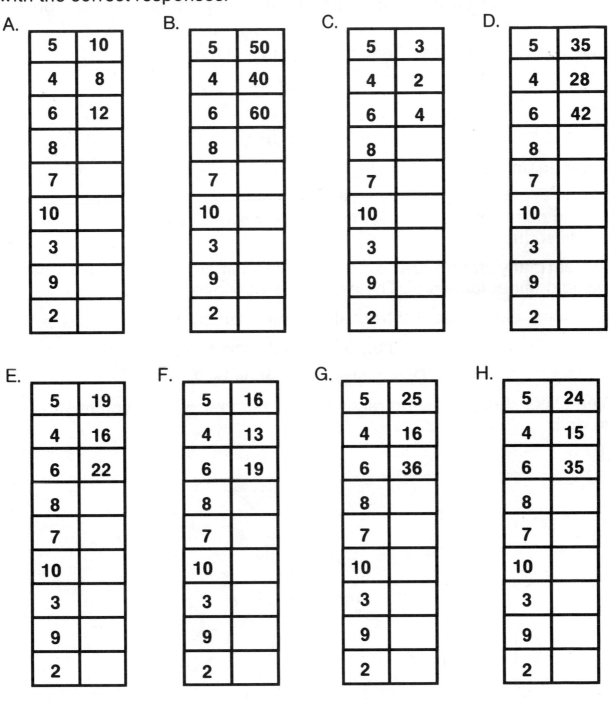

A.

5	10
4	8
6	12
8	
7	
10	
3	
9	
2	

B.

5	50
4	40
6	60
8	
7	
10	
3	
9	
2	

C.

5	3
4	2
6	4
8	
7	
10	
3	
9	
2	

D.

5	35
4	28
6	42
8	
7	
10	
3	
9	
2	

E.

5	19
4	16
6	22
8	
7	
10	
3	
9	
2	

F.

5	16
4	13
6	19
8	
7	
10	
3	
9	
2	

G.

5	25
4	16
6	36
8	
7	
10	
3	
9	
2	

H.

5	24
4	15
6	35
8	
7	
10	
3	
9	
2	

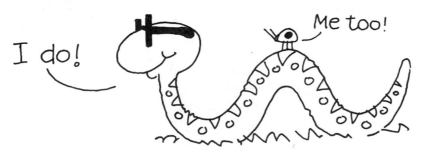

I do!

Me too!

GA1336

Who Sees What I See?

This is your chance to be a teacher. You may now create your own problems.

Your job is to
  First: Decide what your rule will be (+, –, ×, ÷).
  Second: Once you decide on a rule, work out the answers for all nine numerals.
  Third: Write the answers in the boxes for 5, 4 and 6.
  Fourth: Then pass this sheet on to your classmates, and see if they can arrive at your solution.

A.

5	
4	
6	
8	
7	
10	
3	
9	
2	

B.

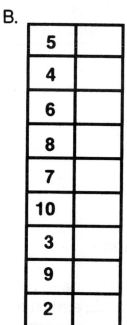

5	
4	
6	
8	
7	
10	
3	
9	
2	

C.

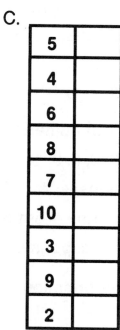

5	
4	
6	
8	
7	
10	
3	
9	
2	

Hey! I'm a teacher!

D.

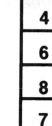

5	
4	
6	
8	
7	
10	
3	
9	
2	

E.

5	
4	
6	
8	
7	
10	
3	
9	
2	

F.

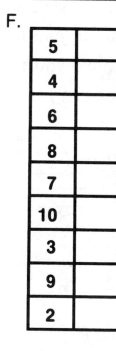

5	
4	
6	
8	
7	
10	
3	
9	
2	

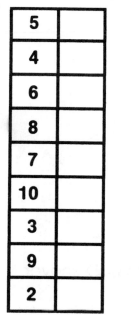

GA1336

M 'N' MS

SKILLS: Gathering and Interpreting Data
Mean, Median, Mode

Mean = Find the average of all the responses.

Median = Place the responses in numerical order and locate the middle response. If the number of responses is even, find the average of the middle pair.

Mode = The most common response

Ask each student to write a number from 1 to 10 on a piece of paper. Gather this information and record it at the chalkboard.

Example:

3, 5, 1, 4, 9, 5, 6, 8, 6, 4, 3, 5, 10

Rewrite the responses in numerical order:

1, 3, 3, 4, 4, 5, 5, 5, 6, 6, 8, 9, 10

mean = 69 ÷ 13 (responses) = 5. 3 mean

median = middle response = 5 median

mode = most common response = 5 mode

Try it again! Gather more information from students in the class. Discover the MEAN, MEDIAN and MODE for each set of responses.

1. How many brothers and sisters do you have?

2. How many rooms are in your house?

3. How many books have you read since the beginning of the year?

*4. How many pancakes can you eat during one meal?

I'll take the mean!

I've got the median!

I did the mode last time!

Career Choice

SKILLS: Computational Skills
Binary System
Place Value

Career Choice will give you the unique ability to accurately know, as well as successfully predict, a classmate's career ambition in life. Have someone in the class choose any one of the fifty careers that can be found on the Career Choice page. This person is not to disclose his/her choice to you. Once the selection is made, have this person examine all of the careers that can be found listed in alphabetical order on this page. They will also see careers listed in six columns headed by the letters A, B, C, D, E and F. The classmate is to tell you only the column or columns in which his/her career choice appears.

For example:

Suppose the Career Choice is a student's wish to become a jockey. This classmate must tell you, not his/her choice but the column or columns that this choice appears in.

"My Career Choice can be found in columns B, D and F."

For you to be able to identify this student's Career Choice, all you have to do is give a numerical value to each column heading as indicated.

A	B	C	D	E	F
32	16	8	4	2	1

In the above illustration, the columns noted were B, D and F. If you use the values assigned to these columns, you will arrive at the following:

B D F
$16 + 4 + 1 = 21$

Now refer to the chart titled Career Choice and you will see that 21 is assigned to the Career Choice of jockey.

I'm gonna be a mechanic!

Tools

GA1336

Career Choice

1. Actor
2. Animal Trainer
3. Archaeologist
4. Architect
5. Artist
6. Author
7. Baker
8. Banker
9. Bus Driver
10. Chef
11. Clergyman
12. Clown
13. Conductor
14. Dentist
15. Designer
16. Doctor
17. Fireman
18. Fisherman
19. Homemaker
20. Inventor
21. Jockey
22. Journalist
23. Landscaper
24. Lawyer
25. Marine
26. Meteorologist
27. Mathematician
28. Mechanic
29. Miner
30. Musician
31. Nurse
32. Photographer
33. Pilot
34. Policeman
35. Politician
36. Race Car Driver
37. Sailor
38. Secretary
39. Shoemaker
40. Shopkeeper
41. Salesperson
42. Social Worker
43. Soldier
44. Tailor
45. Taxi Driver
46. Teacher
47. Travel Agent
48. Truck Driver
49. Veterinarian
50. Waiter/Waitress

Mr. Mouse's Shoe Shop

Shoes Repaired & Polished →

GA1336

Career Choice

A	B	C	D
Photographer	Doctor	Banker	Architect
Pilot	Fireman	Bus Driver	Artist
Policeman	Fisherman	Chef	Author
Politician	Homemaker	Clergyman	Baker
Race Car Driver	Inventor	Clown	Clown
Sailor	Jockey	Conductor	Conductor
Secretary	Journalist	Dentist	Dentist
Shoemaker	Landscaper	Designer	Designer
Shopkeeper	Lawyer	Lawyer	Inventor
Salesperson	Marine	Marine	Jockey
Social Worker	Meteorologist	Meteorologist	Journalist
Soldier	Mathematician	Mathematician	Landscaper
Tailor	Mechanic	Mechanic	Mechanic
Taxi Driver	Miner	Miner	Miner
Teacher	Musician	Musician	Musician
Travel Agent	Nurse	Nurse	Nurse
Truck Driver	Truck Driver	Shopkeeper	Race Car Driver
Veterinarian	Veterinarian	Salesperson	Sailor
Waiter/Waitress	Waiter/Waitress	Social Worker	Secretary
		Soldier	Shoemaker
		Tailor	Tailor
		Taxi Driver	Taxi Driver
		Teacher	Teacher
		Travel Agent	Travel Agent

E

Animal Trainer
Archaeologist
Author
Baker
Chef
Clergyman
Dentist
Designer
Fisherman
Homemaker
Journalist
Landscape
Meteorologist
Mathematician
Musician
Nurse
Policeman
Politician
Secretary
Shoemaker
Social Worker
Soldier
Teacher
Travel Agent
Waiter/Waitress

I'm not cut out to sell insurance.

F

Actor
Archaeologist
Artist
Baker
Bus Driver
Clergyman
Conductor
Designer
Fireman
Homemaker
Jockey
Landscaper
Marine
Mathematician
Miner
Nurse

Pilot
Politician
Sailor
Shoemaker
Salesperson
Soldier
Taxi Driver
Travel Agent
Veterinarian

GA1336

Career Choice

Use the Career Choice list to complete the numerical value distributions of the occupations below.

Name_____

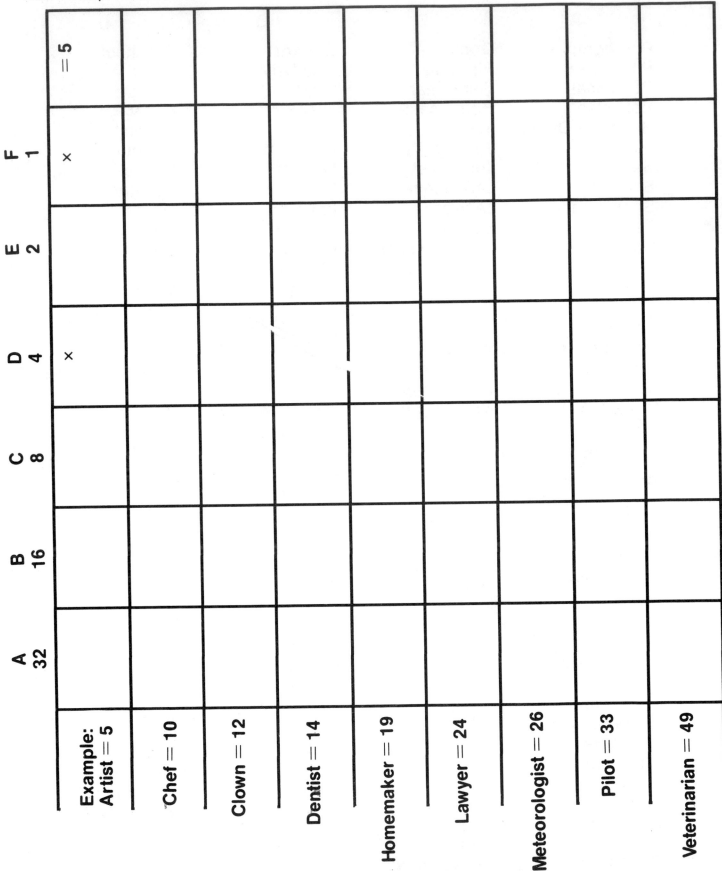

GA1336

E.S.P.

SKILLS: Computation Drill
Integers

Materials: Four sets of cards numbered 1 through 6.
Size of the cards should be 4½″ x 6½″.

Players: Small group or the entire class

Objective: The winning player or team will have the lowest score in the difference column.

How to Play: Three columns of numbers are headed by My Guess, The Card and The Difference. There can be anywhere from five to ten spaces for responses.

Figure 1

My Guess	The Card	The Difference

The number columns should be provided for each player. Example: three players, then three sets of number columns.

The first thing each player does is guess what the top card is in the unexposed deck of cards.

Before the top card is shown, all of the players should write ten numbers, one in each cell in the My Guess column. See Figure 2.

Anybody in there?

ESP

Figure 2 shows the recorded guess of both players before the first of the ten cards is exposed.

Figure 2

Player A

My Guess	The Card	The Difference
3		
2		
2		
4		
6		
3		
1		
4		
5		
4		

Player B

My Guess	The Card	The Difference
4		
3		
4		
2		
1		
6		
5		
3		
2		
3		

How about another game of ESP? — Yer on!

GA1336

Figure 3

Player A

My Guess	The Card	The Difference
3	1	2
2	2	0
2	3	1
4		
6		
3		
1		
4		
5		
4		

Player B

My Guess	The Card	The Difference
4	1	3
3	2	1
4	3	1
2		
1		
6		
5		
3		
2		
3		

Figure 3 shows what to do after the first of the ten cards is exposed.

Suppose the first exposed card is a 1. Record this in The Card column for both teams. In The Difference column Player A records 2; Player B records 3.

Suppose the second card is a 2. Again this is recorded in The Card column for both teams. This time in The Difference column, Player A records O, Player B records 1.

One more example, suppose the third card is 3. Again this is recorded in The Card column for both teams. In The Difference column, Player A records 1 (subtract the smaller number from the larger number). Player B also records a 1 in The Difference column. After ten cards are exposed and the difference is recorded in The Difference column, total the sum of all ten numbers in the last column. The winning player has the lowest score when comparing the sums of these columns. The winner is said to have the better E.S.P. power.

I WON! I WON! I WON!

CLICK!

GA1336

Another possibility when playing E.S.P. is to say the difference between the My Guess and The Card columns. Just subtract and be aware of positive and negative numbers. Record this answer in The Difference column.

My Guess	The Card	The Difference
4	6	-2

If you play the game with integers, once there is a total in The Difference column, the winning team is the team closest to zero.

E.S.P. = EDUCATION SUPPORTS PROGRESS

Education Supports Progress!

GA1336

The Prime Letter Chart

SKILLS: Multiplication Facts Drill
              Prime Numbers
              Prime Factorization

The Prime Letter Chart assigns special number values to all of the letters listed in the chart. The number value given to each letter is a prime number.

The Prime Letter Chart can be used to discover the point values of many different words.

In the space provided below each letter, record the point value of that letter once it is determined that the letter has a point value.

The next step is to multiply the point values (which are prime numbers), and you will arrive at a product.

Prime Letter Chart

A	B	C	D	E	F	H	L	P	R	T
2	2	2	2	3	3	3	5	5	7	11

Example: Find the product of BASIC .

B	A	S	I	C
2	2			2

$= 2 \times 2 \times 2 = \boxed{8}$

Find the product for THANKS .

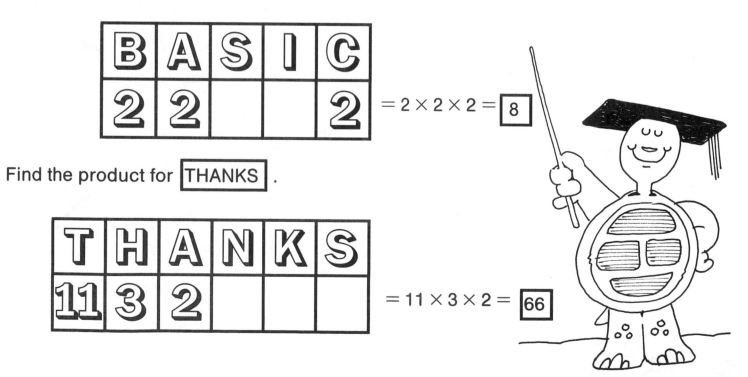

T	H	A	N	K	S
11	3	2			

$= 11 \times 3 \times 2 = \boxed{66}$

GA1336

And still one more example:

Find the product for CONSTITUTION .

C	O	N	S	T	I	T	U	T	I	O	N
2				11		11		11			

$$= 2 \times 11 \times 11 \times 11$$

$$11 \times 11 \times 11 = 1331, \qquad 1331 \times 2 = \boxed{2662}$$

Build on this same Prime Letter Chart theme, only the next time you might want to consider different letters and prime numbers.

GA1336

Prime Letter Chart

D	E	F	I	L	M	O	P	S	T	W
2	2	2	2	3	3	3	5	5	7	11

Find the product for

Your name:

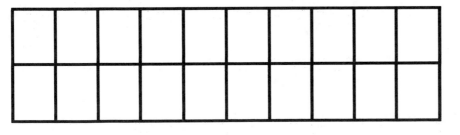

Answer

_____

Your city:

Answer

_____

Your favorite color:

Answer

_____

Your friend, school subject or favorite book:

Answer

_____

GA1336

Left or Right?

SKILLS: Recording Decimals
Reading Decimals

Materials: Numeral cards numbered 0 to 6, three of each card. Direction cards labeled *Left* or *Right*, six of each card.

Players: Two to four players or two teams with two players on each team

Objective: To use the five numeral cards and the five direction cards to create the largest five-digit number

How to Play: Play begins with team A shuffling the numeral cards and drawing five of them facedown. The same team will now shuffle all of the direction cards, draw five of them and lay them facedown.

Sample numeral cards   Sample direction cards

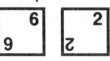   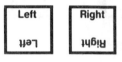

The card measurement for both decks is 2½" x 3½". The interplay between the two teams can be recorded with or without half-inch graph paper. The sample play described is using the graph paper. The graph paper is eleven cells in length with a decimal point in the middle cell.

Figure 1

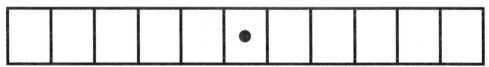

Each player takes a turn with the five numeral cards and the five direction cards.

The player will show a numeral card followed by a direction card. The direction card indicates where and in which cell the player is to record that particular numeral.

Example:

First numeral card

The direction card

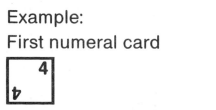

The player or team would record this play as follows:

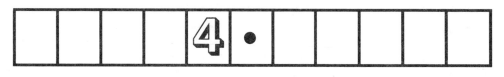

The direction card *left*, indicates the numeral card should be recorded to the left of the decimal point.

Perhaps the next cards drawn for this player:

Second numeral card

The direction card

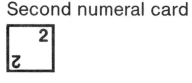   

Play would be recorded:

Third numeral card

The direction card

Play would be recorded:

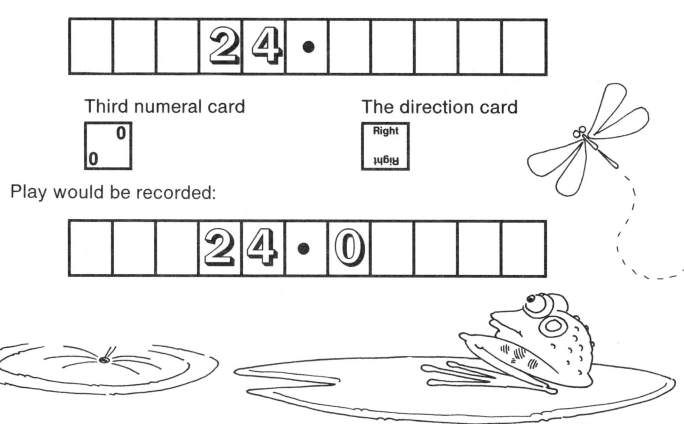

GA1336

Fourth numeral card	The direction card

Play would be recorded:

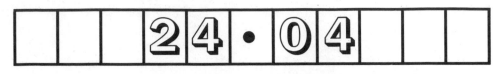

Fifth and final numeral card	The direction card

The final play would be recorded:

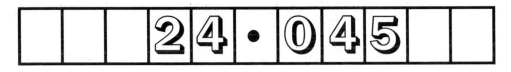

The answer would be read as twenty-four and forty-five thousandths. It is now player or team B's turn to follow the same procedure after shuffling both the entire deck of numeral cards and the entire deck of direction cards.

If this player is able to create a five-digit number that is greater than player A, player B will win the game. If this does not happen, the win belongs to player A.

An extension might be to try for the lowest five-digit number.

GA1336

Brainteaser XI

SKILLS: Problem Solving
Divergent Thought

Materials: Twelve cards measuring 4″ x 6″. The months in the year are individually listed at the top of each card. (illustration below)

How to Play: Place the twelve cards in the following order. May is to be at the top of the pile and the last card is to be March. All of the cards in the pile should be facedown.

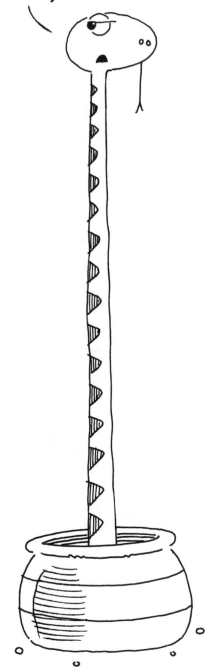

My hood's at the dry cleaners.

May	Sept.	Dec.	July	Feb.	Oct.	April	Jan.	June	August	Nov.	March

Your task is to somehow arrange these cards in their correct sequential calendar order. Before you begin working toward a solution to the Brainteaser, show the class the order of the cards as shown above. Tell the class that you will reassemble the twelve cards in the correct order.

As you hold all twelve cards, begin by spelling *January*. As you call each letter in the month, you must place the card from the top of the pile on the bottom of the pile. When spelling *January*, you will call seven letters. After calling each letter, you must place the card on top and move it to the bottom of the pile. The very next card (in this instance it will be the eight card) is ready for you to show to the class. It will be ⬜January⬜. Take ⬜January⬜ out of the pile and the pile will now have eleven cards.

Repeat the above procedure, only this time you will spell *February*. As long as you carefully place the cards in the prescribed order, (remember to remove the very next card after you spell the month) all twelve months will line up in their proper sequential order.

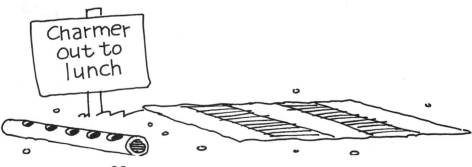

Charmer out to lunch

GA1336

Brainteaser XII

SKILLS: Problem Solving

In each of the sentences below is a challenge for you. In each sentence the math word is carefully hidden. Allow yourself fifteen minutes to see how many of the hidden words you can uncover. Each sentence contains one math word.

Example:

    1. Have you met Erica before?   The math word is <u>met Er</u>.

    2. We all know that those conditions were perfect. The math word is <u>se cond</u>.

Try your skill at the following thirty sentences. Use the scoring range to determine how well you have done.

              25-30 . . . . super

              20-24 . . . . great

              15-19 . . . . good

              10-14 . . . . not bad

1. Is it a well-known fact or not?   _____

2. My good friend Selma thinks about her art.   _____

3. It is my hope rational thoughts will prevail.   _____

4. The pepper center of the world is on the East Coast.   _____

5. The Isle of Capri meets all of our expectations.   _____

HEY! I'M "SUPER!"

30 SUPER!

GA1336

Brainteaser XII

6. To stop the tumult, I plead for unity. _____

7. The musical group Purple Haze rocked the huge crowd. _____

8. I'm glad dedication is honorable. _____

9. We are sure a son lives at home. _____

10. Remember to bring the flowers home, Diana! _____

11. The new movie star Ray Smith came to town. _____

12. Brett went yesterday. _____

13. We will stay later, also. _____

14. Can you teach me tricks like that? _____

15. He sang lead tenor until yesterday. _____

16. I would like to teach art after school. _____

17. The small cub eats many times a day. _____

18. Will Maude crease her dress? _____

19. They will trade green chips for blue ones. _____

20. Robyn will be in India, Monday. _____

Brainteaser XII

21. If you dig it out, be sure you do it quickly. _____

22. Chad is covering the sculpture with a blanket. _____

23. Charles slept through eight meetings. _____

24. Sometimes to be lax is to be forgetful. _____

25. A small tot always sleeps many hours. _____

26. You can see Tess elated when the phone rings. _____

27. When pigs eat slop, everything smells. _____

28. Keep ice cream in the freezer. _____

29. When we win, cheering is quite obvious. _____

30. The sharp tempo interests many students. _____

Try creating some of your own sentences. Remember, hide the math word!

1. _____

2. _____

3. _____

Wake up, Charles!

1, 2, 3, 4

SKILLS: Equations
        Basic Facts

What do you know about the numerals

Super thinkers should be able to list at least ten different discoveries that relate to these four numerals.

Some examples might be:

a.

a. 1, 2 and 4 are all factors of 4.

b. Using these four digits, the largest four-digit number that can be written is **4321**.

c. The numerals **1** and **4** are made up of only straight lines.

d. **1** and **2** are made up of three letters each. one = **1**, two = **2**

List all of your discoveries and compare them to the answers on the next page.

GA1336

1 2 3 4

Discoveries for the 1, 2, 3, 4 knowledge test.

1. The sum of the four digits is 10.

2. The digital root (a single digit) is equal to 1.

$$1 + 2 + 3 + 4 = 10 = 1 + 0 = 1$$

3. The numerals 2 and 3 are prime numbers.

4. The numeral 4 is the only composite number.

5. The numeral 4 is a multiple of 2.

6. There are two odd numerals 1 and 3.

7. There are two even numerals 2 and 4.

8. If you multiply $4 \times 3 \times 2 \times 1$, the answer is 24 or 4 factorial. The sign for 4 factorial is 4!

9. The numeral 4 is the product of the square of 2 or $2^2 = 4$.

10. The numeral 2 is the only even prime number.

GA1336

A.K.A. 54

SKILLS: Computational Skills
               Fractions
               Operations

Rather than addressing each student by his/her given name, an interesting as well as open-ended change of pace happens when the class is involved in this activity. The activity begins and ends with a number. This number is a specific number that will identify a particular student.

For example, CHRIS WARD will be known as 54.

The ten's place numeral is derived from the number of letters in the student's first name and the ones place numeral is derived from the number of letters in the student's last name.

Again . . . . CHRIS WARD
                  5   4   = 54

RYAN CAMERON = 47

MICHELE WOOD = 74

MATTHEW MCNEIL = 76

ALLISON BROWNING = 78

Before initiating this activity, the teacher should instruct the class as to the particular math concept they should be aware of during a given time.

GA1336

Let the students know if they are to consider place value, then CHRIS WARD = 54

          . . . addition, then CHRIS WARD = 9

          . . . subtraction, then CHRIS WARD = 1

          . . . multiplication, then CHRIS WARD = 20

          . . . fractions, then CHRIS WARD = 5/4 or 1¼

Perhaps you might want to carry this idea somewhat further . . .

   a. RYAN CAMERON with MATTHEW MCNEIL = 123, why?
      [47 + 76 = 123]

   b. Write a few numbers on the chalkboard and have the class identify the students.

GA1336

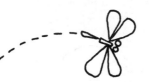

A.K.A. 54

Complete this chart by using your first and last name and answering each problem according to:

Place Value	first name last name _____ _____ tens ones _____ _____	= _____
Multiplication	first name last name _____ _____ × _____ _____	= _____
Subtraction	first name last name _____ _____ − _____ _____	= _____
Addition	first name last name _____ _____ + _____ _____	= _____
Fraction	first name _____ last name _____ $\dfrac{\Box}{\Box}$	= _____

GA1336

I'll Take a Half!

SKILLS: Geometry
            Binary System
            Fractions

The word *half* can and will conjure up many different images in someone's mind, but the concept of *half* will remain a constant.

A half will divide something into two parts; however, the two parts will be two equal parts.

You can experiment with this idea by using a sheet of paper, 8″ x 10″, and labeling it as a unit.

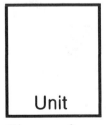

Unit

Figure A

Step 1: Fold the unit sheet in half. As you do this, make sure that you have a definite straight line crease in the paper.

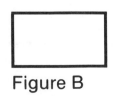

Figure B

Step 2: Take this new shape (Figure B) and FOLD IT IN HALF. Once again and throughout this activity, every time you fold the paper it is important that you have a straight line crease.

Figure C

Step 3: Figure C folded in half will produce Figure D.

Figure D

If you relate Figure D to Figure C, you can see that Figure D is half of Figure C. You should also be able to see that Figure D is a fourth of Figure B and an eighth of Figure A.

Step 4: At this point, if you unfold the sheet of 8″ x 10″ paper, it should look something like Figure E.

The original unit was folded in half three times. (Figure E). Each fold was followed with a straight line crease.

Figure E

Hey! This is more fun than a roll in the mud!

49

GA1336

The problem for you now to consider is . . .

Start with a new sheet of 8" x 10" paper. Can you fold this unit sheet in half . . . seven times?

*Remember, a straight line crease after each fold.

Some questions to consider . . . .

- Would it help if you began the folding process with a larger size unit sheet of paper?
- Could you do it if you used thinner paper?

If the idea of folding a sheet of paper seven or eight times and each fold requiring a straight line crease is difficult and even physically impossible to do, the power of one's mind is absolutely awesome.

Consider the following: A unit folded in half, and then folded in half again and again and again and so on into infinity.

After the first fold, the unit would be in half. After the second fold, the unit would be in fourths, followed by eighths.

Perhaps the following concentration on denominators will help you to predict the size of future folds.

1	$\frac{1}{2}$	$\frac{1}{4}$	$\frac{1}{8}$	$\frac{1}{16}$	$\frac{1}{32}$

What would be the size of the next five folds?

Are you making spitwads again?

No. . .I'm trying to fold this into infinity!

GA1336

Last One Wins!

SKILLS: Basic Multiplication Facts

Materials: Two special number cubes.
One cube is numbered 9, 8, 7, 6, 5, 4.
The second cube is numbered 1, 2, 3, 4, 5, 6.

Players: The entire class or two to five students in a small group

Objective: To win, there should be one product cell remaining on the chalkboard and your name should appear in that cell.

How to Play: Reproduce the following gameboard on the chalkboard:

54	48	45	42	40
36	35	32	30	28
27	25	24	21	20
18	16	14	12	9
8	7	6	5	4

The numeral in each cell represents a product that a player can arrive at when tossing the two special number cubes described above. Before play is to begin, members of the class should each select one of the gameboard products and write his/her name in that particular product cell.

Now that's my kind of race!

ZOOOO OOOOOOMM

Finish Line ←

GA1336

Hmm..."Craig" would be a nice name if it's a boy.

Example:

54 Craig	48 Jerry	45 Alan	42 Michele	40 Polly
36 June	35 Dawn	32 Matthew	30 Russell	28 Kelli
27 Veda	25 John	24 Ms. James	21 Dana	20 Andre
18 William	16 Judy	14 Robyn	12 Aaron	9 Andrew
8 Cory	7 Robert	6 Qiana	5 Steven	4 Amanda

Once the cells have been claimed by the students, be sure that you, the teacher, also claim a product cell.

Each player will now take three chances at tossing the number cubes. The number on the top face of each cube will become a factor. Multiply the factors to reach a product. Once the product is correctly identified, the teacher is to erase all markings (product and player's name) in that cell.

$$8 \times 4 = 32$$

On the gameboard both the numeral (32) and the person's name (Matthew) should be erased. The cubes will move from player to player until there is only one name and one product remaining. In other words, *last one wins*!

*If you play this game with two to five players, allow each participant to select up to five product cells. Play will then be the same as described above.

Color Words

Color me "yellow."

SKILLS: Addition Facts
Multiplication Facts
Equations
Properties

Use Color Words as one alternative approach to help students with the understanding and application of basic multiplication and addition facts. Color all of the words on the Color Word page. After this has been completed, cut and paste the color words onto separate cards. Doing this will greatly emphasize the use of this teaching aid.

Before the class, hold up the various color cards:

How many letters in **red** ? Color me "red."

How many letters in **blue** ?

How many letters in **red** + **blue** ?

When using the color words with multiplication facts,

red represents the 3 times table.

blue represents the 4 times table.

green, **white**, **black** and **brown**

each represents the 5 times table.

orange, **purple** and **yellow** each represents the 6 times table.

All of this makes for some very interesting and creative ideas.

GA1336

Again, before the class:

How many letters do you think of when I say **blue**, **blue**, **blue** ?

How many letters do you think of when I say **blue** 7 times?

How many letters come into your mind when I say

(3 times **white**) plus (2 times **orange**)?

Use of this alternative approach will allow you to develop the concept of equations.

(8 times **yellow**) plus (2 times **red**)

$(8 \times 6) + (2 \times 3) =$

([6 times **green**] plus **white**) minus **blue**

$([6 \times 5] + 5) - 4 =$

Color me orange!

Color me white!

54

Color Words

Answer these color word equations.

A. (4 times **purple**) minus **black** = _____ letters	B. **yellow** plus **brown** plus **red** = _____ letters
C. **red** plus (2 times **yellow**) = _____ letters	D. 7 times **orange** = _____ letters
E. **blue** times **red** = _____ letters	F. **orange** times **green** = _____ letters
G. (6 times **black**) minus **blue** = _____ letters	H. (**purple** times **white**) minus **red** = _____ letters
I. (**green** times **green**) = _____ letters	J. (**red** times **red**) plus **orange** = _____ letters

55

white	yellow	brown
green	purple	red
blue	orange	black

56

GA1336

Yellow Jack

SKILLS: Improper Fractions
       Mixed Numbers

Materials: Twenty-one playing cards (4″ x 6″)
Distribution of the cards: $\frac{1}{8}$ 5 cards, $\frac{2}{8}$ 4 cards, $\frac{3}{8}$ 4 cards, $\frac{4}{8}$ 4 cards, $\frac{5}{8}$ 1 card, $\frac{6}{8}$ 1 card, $\frac{7}{8}$ 1 card, $\frac{8}{8}$ 1 card

Object: The game winner is the team with the most scoring at the game's end. Each team will take three turns.

How to Play: Yellow Jack is for two to four players. In turn, each player will shuffle the playing cards and then draw six cards from the top of the unexposed deck. The cards are then exposed one at a time. Each player will record the number of yellow fractional parts shown on each of the cards. After all of the cards are exposed, the total of the yellow parts is first written as an improper fraction and then to a whole or mixed number. This total is then to be measured with the scoring range.

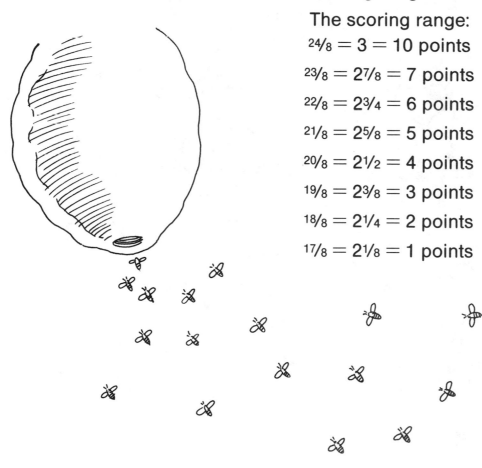

The scoring range:

$\frac{24}{8} = 3 = 10$ points

$\frac{23}{8} = 2\frac{7}{8} = 7$ points

$\frac{22}{8} = 2\frac{3}{4} = 6$ points

$\frac{21}{8} = 2\frac{5}{8} = 5$ points

$\frac{20}{8} = 2\frac{1}{2} = 4$ points

$\frac{19}{8} = 2\frac{3}{8} = 3$ points

$\frac{18}{8} = 2\frac{1}{4} = 2$ points

$\frac{17}{8} = 2\frac{1}{8} = 1$ points

57

GA1336

Any scoring greater than $\frac{24}{8}$ will not be given any points. Any scoring less than $\frac{17}{8}$ will also not be awarded any points.

Follow this sample play:

After Player A draws the top six cards, he/she should record on paper...

Record

first card $\frac{1}{8}$ .... $\frac{1}{8}$

second card $\frac{1}{8}$ .... $\frac{2}{8}$

third card $\frac{6}{8}$ .... $\frac{8}{8}$

fourth card $\frac{2}{8}$ .... $\frac{10}{8}$

fifth card $\frac{2}{8}$ .... $\frac{12}{8}$

sixth card $\frac{7}{8}$ .... $\frac{19}{8}$

$\frac{19}{8} = 2\frac{3}{8}$. According to the scoring range, $\frac{19}{8}$ is equal to 3 scoring points. Player B will then shuffle all twenty-one cards and draw the top six cards.

Hey! Let's play Yellow Jack!

Great idea!

58

GA1336

Player B's objective is to score higher in the scoring range than Player A. Either player must not surpass $^{24}/_8$. Each player or team will have three attempts at scoring. At the end of the three rounds, the game winner will have the most points.

59

Yellow Jack Playing Cards (2½" x 3½")

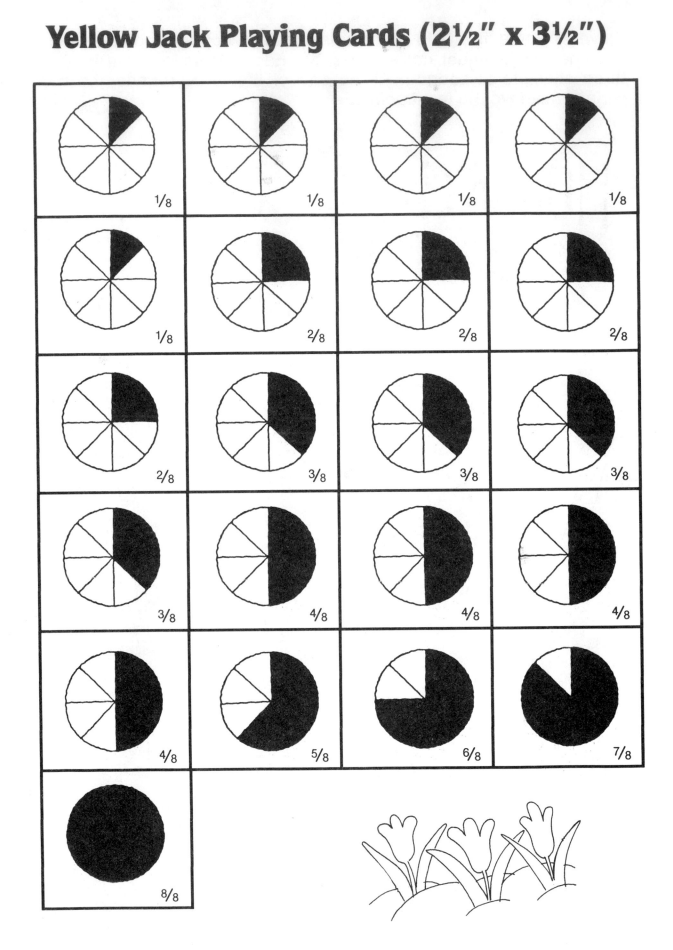

GA1336

Any Way You Look at It!

SKILLS: Addition
Renaming
Palindromes
Interpreting Data

The question to be answered is . . .
How many palindromic dates occur in a year?

Palindromes are numerals that read the same from right to left or left to right.

424, 1331, 14641, 823328

The following point of reference will help you in your discovery toward reaching a solution to this problem.

1. When recording dates that occur during the first nine months of the year, use three digits.

   January 14 . . . written in digits . . . 114
   March 19 319
   September 10 910

2. When recording dates that occur during the last three months of the year, use four digits.

   October 9 . . . written in digits . . . 1009
   November 26 1126
   *December 21 1221

The chart on the next page lists the twelve months. Consider and record all palindromic dates below each month.

*a palindromic date

What's a palindromic date!

I dunno... I never eat dates.

GA1336

Palindromic Dates for Each Month

Jan.	Feb.	Mar.	Apr.	May	June	July	Aug.	Sept.	Oct.	Nov.	Dec.

How many palindromic dates occur each year? _____

Something to think about. . .

Palindromic dates also have palindromic times.

Example: May 15 = 515; times—5:15 a.m., 5:15 p.m.

Can you find more dates like these?

Any Way You Look at It!

Palindrome?
Could be
some kind
of a
camel...

Find palindromic numbers for these dates.

Remember, some of these may take more than one step to reach the palindrome.

September 18	August 26	November 15
March 29	**August 29**	**Your Birthday**

GA1336

The Awesome Power of 2

SKILLS: Binary System
Divergent Thinking

Pretend. Just suppose that one day each year is set aside and is known as the Day of the Time Blox. A Time Blox is something that looks somewhat like a star (★). Because its characteristics are so unusual, the TIME BLOX is a very valuable commodity. The most unique trait enjoyed by TIME BLOX is its ability to clone itself. It is interesting that the TIME BLOX performs this function just one day during the year. The function of cloning begins during the first hour of that particular day. It is during this first hour that the TIME BLOX will clone itself and actually double in number. For the second hour and for the remaining hours of the day, the TIME BLOX continues this process.

With this ability to reproduce itself, you might begin to wonder about the idea of having 1 TIME BLOX for the first hour of the day followed by 2 TIME BLOX at the end of the second hour, 4 TIME BLOX at the end of the third hour. The problem to be considered is "How many TIME BLOX will there be at the end of this very special day?"

Time Blox

★   = 1

Time Blox

★★   = 2

Time Blox

= 256

★ ★ ★ ★ ★ ★ ★ ★ ★ ★   ★ ★ ★ ★ ★ ★ ★ ★ ★ ★
★ ★ ★ ★ ★ ★ ★ ★ ★ ★   ★ ★ ★ ★ ★ ★ ★ ★ ★ ★
★ ★ ★ ★ ★ ★ ★ ★ ★ ★   ★ ★ ★ ★ ★ ★ ★ ★ ★ ★
★ ★ ★ ★ ★ ★ ★ ★ ★ ★   ★ ★ ★ ★ ★ ★ ★ ★ ★ ★
★ ★ ★ ★ ★ ★ ★ ★ ★ ★   ★ ★ ★ ★ ★ ★ ★ ★ ★ ★
★ ★ ★ ★ ★ ★ ★ ★ ★ ★   ★ ★ ★ ★ ★ ★ ★ ★ ★ ★
★ ★ ★ ★ ★ ★ ★ ★ ★ ★   ★ ★ ★ ★ ★ ★ ★ ★ ★ ★
★ ★ ★ ★ ★ ★ ★ ★ ★ ★   ★ ★ ★ ★ ★ ★ ★ ★ ★ ★

★ ★ ★ ★ ★ ★ ★ ★ ★ ★   ★ ★ ★ ★ ★ ★ ★ ★ ★ ★
★ ★ ★ ★ ★ ★ ★ ★ ★ ★   ★ ★ ★ ★ ★ ★ ★ ★ ★ ★
★ ★ ★ ★ ★ ★ ★ ★ ★ ★   ★ ★ ★ ★ ★ ★ ★ ★ ★ ★
★ ★ ★ ★ ★ ★ ★ ★ ★ ★   ★ ★ ★ ★ ★ ★ ★ ★ ★ ★
★ ★ ★ ★ ★ ★ ★ ★ ★ ★   ★ ★ ★ ★ ★ ★ ★ ★ ★ ★
★ ★ ★ ★ ★ ★ ★ ★ ★ ★   ★ ★ ★ ★ ★ ★ ★ ★ ★ ★
★ ★ ★ ★ ★ ★ ★ ★ ★ ★   ★ ★ ★ ★ ★ ★ ★ ★ ★ ★
★ ★ ★ ★ ★ ★ ★ ★ ★ ★   ★ ★ ★ ★ ★ ★ ★ ★ ★ ★

What are you doing, Harold? Watching Time Blox double.

Name_____

Time Blox

Fill in the number of Time Blox for each hour.

Remember, the amount of Time Blox will double in number during each hour.

1st hour	2nd hour	3rd hour	4th hour	5th hour	6th hour
= 1	= 2				
7th hour	8th hour	9th hour	10th hour	11th hour	12th hour
		= 256			
13th hour	14th hour	15th hour	16th hour	17th hour	18th hour
19th hour	20th hour	21st hour	22nd hour	23rd hour	24th hour

* If you can show 256 Time Blox (9th hour) on a sheet of 8″ x 10″ paper, how many sheets of 8″ x 10″ paper will you need to show Time Blox at the end of the 24th hour?

_____ sheets of 8″ x 10″ paper

GA1336

Close to 39!

SKILLS: Basic Skills
Problem Solving

How old are you?

Close to 39.

Start   **Start**

3	1	9	5	2	6
2	0	8	4	1	3
5	7	8	2	0	1
4	2	3	5	7	9
6	1	2	5	3	3
8	5	9	4	2	6

Start   **Start**

Create your own number path. The objective is to get as close to a sum of 39 as you possibly can. You may start at any corner.

You must accomplish this task in ten moves or less.

A major rule is that you may never stop on a number if the sum is a multiple of ⬜ 5.

Follow this play . . . .

```
3  1  9  5  2  6        3 + 0 + 5 + 4 + 6 + 1 + 9 + 5 + 3 + 3 = 39
2  0  8  4  1  3
5  7  8  2  0  1        9 moves
4  2  3  5  7  9
6  1  2  5  3  3
8  5  9  4  2  6
```

A Winning Trail

SKILLS: Basic Facts

Materials: Three cubes—two of the cubes should be numbered 1 through 6.
One cube made up of the following shapes:

A mover for each player

Object: The game winner is the first player or team to reach the end of the trail.

Players: For two to four players

How to Play: The game is played with three cubes. In turn, each player tosses the number cubes first. Once the face numbers at the tops of the cubes are determined, the player then tosses the shape cube. This cube will determine the operation to be performed by the player.

□ = The player will add the numbers on the top face of each cube.

△ = The player will subtract the smaller number from the larger number.

○ = The player will multiply the numbers on the top face of each cube.

▭ = The player will divide the smaller number into the larger number.

end of the trail

GA1336

Player A will place his/her mover on the first space next to Start. Once the operation is determined and then performed on the numbers on the face of both cubes, Player A is to move that number of spaces.

Example:

| 6 | 3 |

If the top face of the shape cube is a

☐ , then 6 + 3 = 9 space move

△ , then 6 – 3 = 3 space move

◯ , then 6 × 3 = 18 space move

▭ , then 6 ÷ 3 = 2 space move

The gameboard has happy faces ☺ . These tell the player to move forward three spaces if the player stops on them.

Sad faces ☹ tell the player to move backward one space again, if the player stops on them.

*Important Rule: If a player tosses | 6 | 6 | , this player must go back to Start and begin play all over.

When Player A completes his/her turn, the cubes are given to Player B. Players alternate turns.

*If the players are not ready for multiplication or division, make the shape cube with two shapes:

☐   ☐   ☐   △   △   △
+   +   +   –   –   –

steep Climb Ahead

When it comes to trails you really pick the winners!

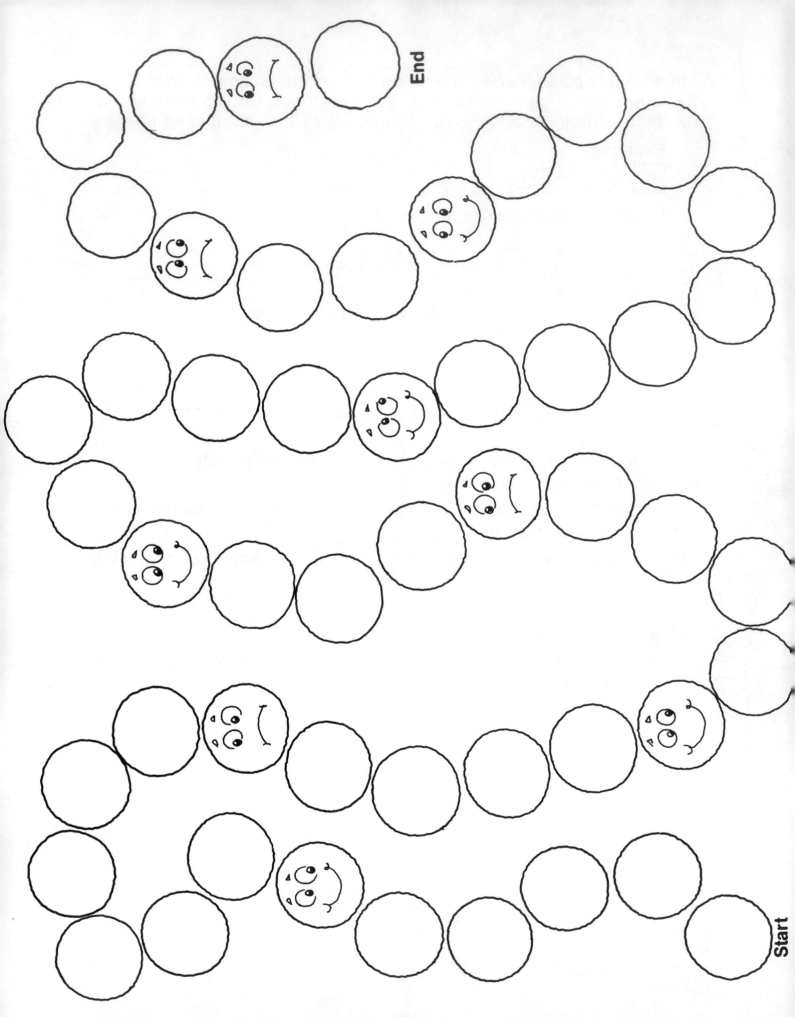

End

Start

72

Teacher for a Day . . .
Well at Least for Ten Minutes!

For a refreshingly creative and enlightening classroom experience, the following is one that will offer you insight as to what takes place in your classroom. It is a unique perspective that will allow you to witness firsthand not only what your students have learned but which of these understandings have been meaningful to them.

Ask for a student volunteer whose job it will be to teach a ten-minute lesson to the entire class. You select a topic that has been previously taught to your students. Allow the student volunteer a day or two preparation time for his/her presentation.

*Be ready for many, many pleasant surprises.

You will get insight as to your own teaching style. You will see first-hand things that your students perceive as being important. You will probably hear almost as many references to affective goals, such as positive self-esteem, as you will to the cognitive references that deal with your instructional objectives.

This is an amazing experience that will give you an opportunity to visualize yourself . . . teaching. It is almost like watching yourself teach while you are seated behind a one-way mirror. You will find yourself actually critiquing your own teaching style.

Don't be surprised by the number of times you hear your volunteer student teacher come out with phrases such as, "Nice try! I knew you could do it! Great job; be proud of yourself!"

*Be ready for many, many pleasant surprises.

..turn to page 53 in your history books... for the next ten minutes we'll be discussing the rise and fall of the Roman Empire...

He sounds just like me!

Action Drill

SKILLS: Operations on Whole Numbers

clap	frown
hop	wink
smile	bow
blink	snap

Action Drill Board

The Action Drill Board is made up of eight spaces with an action word in each space. The student's task is to perform a specific Action Word. The designated Action Word will follow a pattern of exact positioning on the Action Drill Board. The chart will have one X in it at a time. Check the position of the X on the chart and locate the same position on the board. This will indicate the correct Action Drill Word.

Example:

clap	frown
hop	wink
smile	bow
blink	snap

Action Drill Board

A

B

C

Action Drill Chart
A = smile

Action Drill Chart
B = clap

Action Drill Chart
C = wink

wink!

GA1336

Both the Action Drill Board and the Action Drill Chart should be taped to the chalkboard.

Once this is completed, the activity requires an Action Drill Number Fact Board and an Action Drill Number Fact Chart.

Example: 2

8 − 5	3 + 2
4 + 3	9 − 8
2 + 7	6 ÷ 2
7 − 6	4 × 2

Action Drill Number Fact Board

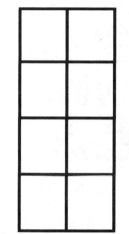

Action Drill Number Fact Chart

Tape the Number Fact Board below the Action Drill Board and tape the Number Fact Drill below the Action Drill Number Fact Chart.

Looking at Example 2

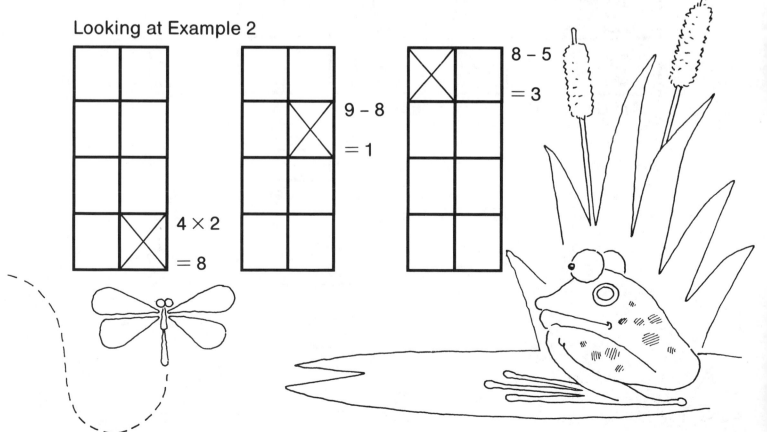

4×2
$= 8$

$9 - 8$
$= 1$

$8 - 5$
$= 3$

GA1336

Once the class becomes aware of what the placement of the X is all about, creative drill will begin.

clap	frown
hop	wink
smile	bow
blink	snap

Action Drill Board

= smile

8 – 5	3 + 2
4 + 3	9 – 8
2 + 7	6 ÷ 2
7 – 6	4 × 2

Action Drill Number Fact Board

= 8 – 5 = 3

smile 3 times

Position of the X will tell the student to [smile], (8 – 5), 3 times.

The activity can be kept open-ended by daily changing the facts on the Action Drill Number Fact Board.

snap!

GA1336

clap	frown
hop	wink
smile	bow
blink	snap

Action Drill Board

Photocopy this page. Use magic markers to color in the Action Words.

That's not fair! Snakes can't wink!

77

Bunches 'N' Bunches

SKILLS: Multiples

Materials: Twenty-four cards (2½" x 3½") numbered 1 through 6. The set is to contain four cards of each numeral.

Players: For two players or an entire class divided into two teams

How to Play: The winning team will score the most points at the end of play. Points are awarded for creating multiples of certain numbers.

This one looks like a bunch of fun!

> A multiple is the product of a given number and a whole number.

> You might also think of multiples as making bunches of a particular product.

> 6, 12, 18, 42, 60, 102 are multiples of 6

> 10, 20, 50, 80, 140, 560 are multiples of 10

In turn, each player will shuffle all twenty-four cards and then take ten cards from the top of the unexposed deck. Each card will be exposed one at a time. Players will score points when the exposed card (shown one at a time) creates a multiple. It may have been decided that points will be awarded for multiples of 4.

For example:

> The ten cards should be lined up on the ledge of the chalkboard. The number side of the card should be unexposed. As each card is exposed, the total is added to reach a sum. Points are scored for the team if the sum is (in this instance) a multiple of 4.

The ten cards in a line at the chalkboard:

One at a time, expose each card and find the sum.

If the first card is a 6 and the second card is a 5, the sum is 11. 11 is not a multiple of 4. Suppose the third card is a 1. The sum of the three cards is 12. A point is scored since 12 is a multiple of 4. This process continues until all ten cards are exposed. Points are scored when any of the sums reaches a multiple of 4.

Once the scoring is completed, the cards are reshuffled and given to Player B.

Another way of scoring points is to predetermine positional values:

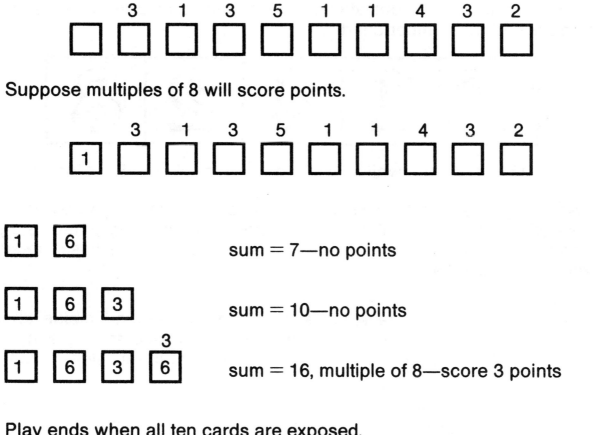

Suppose multiples of 8 will score points.

Play ends when all ten cards are exposed.

GA1336

Color Math Age Chart

SKILLS: Mental Math
           Computational Skills
           Exponents/Binary System

Have someone in class choose a member of his/her family who is twenty-six years of age or younger. This student is to write the family member's age on the chalkboard. Everyone, except the teacher, will now know the mystery person's age. Once the mystery age is known it should be erased from the chalkboard. Now ask the students to concentrate their thoughts on the mystery person's age. The students should look at the number chart and then tell you *all of the colors* that the selected number appears in.

As the colors are cited, commit them to your memory. After noting all of these colors, turn your attention to the *five colors in the lower left-hand row* of the number chart.

16 = red   1 = white   4 = green   2 = yellow   8 = blue

The ability to know the mystery age becomes clear to you when you take all of the colors that were mentioned in the mystery person's age, convert these to numbers, and numbers to a sum. In this case the sum will be the secret age.

For example:
     Suppose someone says, "My sister's age can be found in blue, green and yellow." Your task is to remember that blue = 8, green = 4 and yellow = 2 (8 + 4 + 2). The total of 14 is the mystery person's age. (14)

     Another example:
     red, green, yellow = (16 + 4 + 2) = 22

It would be best to photocopy the age chart and give a copy to each student. The student will then color each numeral according to the letter code.

R = red, W = white, G = Green, B = blue

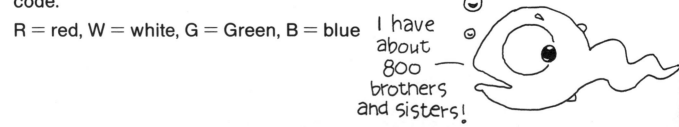

I have about 800 brothers and sisters!

                              GA1336

Color Math Age Chart

(Up to 26 Years Old!)

I'm still a teenager.

9 W	13 W	6 Y	12 G	8 Y	7 W
3 W	11 W	23 R	10 Y	21 W	25 B
17 W	20 G	7 G	15 Y	14 Y	23 G
26 B	15 G	8 R	24 B	5 W	17 R
9 B	3 Y	11 Y	14 G	25 W	21 G
14 B	24 R	22 G	10 B	7 Y	8 B
5 G	12 B	13 G	15 W	22 Y	2 Y
20 R	19 Y	26 Y	6 G	19 W	4 G
25 R	23 W	22 R	11 B	26 R	1 W
9 R	15 B	21 Y	13 B	23 Y	6 R

GA1336

Color Math with Food

SKILLS: Computational Skills
Place Value
Binary System
Problem Solving

Color Math with Food is an exciting as well as a highly motivating activity for both teacher and student. Participants will find themselves in very active classroom roles.

The concept of base two is a central theme to the ideas presented throughout this activity. The following colors are equated with their respective numerals:

$$red = 16$$
$$blue = 8$$
$$green = 4$$
$$yellow = 2$$
$$white = 1$$

These are the only instructions that should be committed to memory. Once you do this, the activity is open-ended.

For example:

"Yesterday I had lunch and if you think about it, lunches come in different colors, so it is quite possible that the lunch I ate yesterday had a number value of 6 points.

It would seem that whatever it was that I ate for my lunch had to be in two colors and the sum total of these two colors was 6 points and that the two colors had to be green and yellow!

Hmmm . . . What did I eat for lunch?"

Possibilities . . . peas and corn
or scrambled egg with green pepper
or spinach with butter or . . . ?

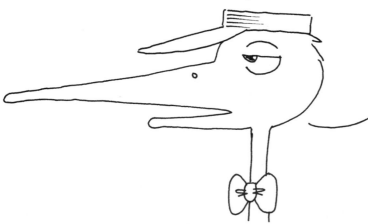

I'll have a Blue, Red, Green, Yellow and White salad bar and a small root beer...

GA1336

It is now open to the students to consider various foods, to relate the food to a color and to relate the color to its respective number value.

Example:
    milk = 1
    butter = 2
    spinach = 4
    blueberries = 8
    tomatoes = 16

This now allows the class an opportunity to design their own 17-point lunch. And you can add still another dimension to this activity. Why not title the activity "The 17-Point, Yucky Lunch!"

Students are to think of different combinations of food. Its color value is 17 points and its appetite appeal is yucky!

Some examples:
                mashed potatoes topped with strawberries
                                    or
            vanilla ice cream topped with hot stewed tomatoes

A nice idea would be to set aside a bulletin board in the class and label it "A Most Yucky Lunch!"

I'll have the vanilla ice cream, topped with hot stewed tomatoes.

Menu

GA1336

Color Math with Food

Complete the following Color Math problems with your own ideas of a "yucky lunch."

Remember the color values: red = 16, blue = 8, green = 4, yellow = 2, white = 1

A. 19 points	B. 7 points
C. 14 points	D. 21 points
E. 18 points	F. 20 points

Flies again!
What a
yucky lunch!

GA1336

How Close Did You Get?

SKILLS: Estimation
           Basic Computational Skills

You will need two sheets of paper, page A and page B. The sample grid as shown in Figure 1 should be copied by each class member on page A.

Problem	My Guess	The Answer	I Missed by. . .
1			
2			
3			
4			

Figure 1

On the second sheet of paper (page B), ask each student to record his/her choice of any numeral from 1 to 10. With perhaps twenty-one students in the class and if the teacher joins in, it is possible to receive twenty-two bits of information.

On page A, the paper with the grid, each participant must make a guess as to the total of *all the responses of all the participants combined*.

For example, if someone thinks that this *combined total* received from all twenty-two participants will be 158, then this is the number that should be recorded in the first space under the heading "My Guess." It represents the estimate that the participant thinks will be the *total response from everyone*. This number should be kept secret until called for at the end of the activity.

GA1336

In order to arrive at this combined total, the leader should ask each person the number he/she wrote as his/her choice from 1 to 10. This information should be on page B.

This is accomplished by allowing each class member the opportunity to respond aloud with his/her recorded selection.

Have a member of the class record each individual response, as it is given, at the chalkboard. Once the total is determined for the entire group, this amount should be recorded on the grid, in the column headed The Answer.

The next step is to have each individual find the difference between the two columns and record this answer in the third column, "I Missed by . . . ."

The winner of the activity will have the lowest difference in the final column.

The activity might run more smoothly if you subtract the smaller number from the larger number in either column.

86

GA1336

Some additional questions:

1. If you waited on tables at a restaurant, how many dishes would you break in a month? (5 to 20)

2. How many A's will you get on your report card?

3. How many blueberry muffins could you eat for breakfast?

4. How many times did you shop or take a trip to a mall last month?

5. How many times did you shop or take a trip to a mall last year?

87

3-D Bingo

BINGO!

SKILLS: Basic Facts
Place Value
Fractions
Equivalent Fractions
Geometric Shapes
Money
Time

Materials: Eight gameboards (8″ x 10″), a set of calling cards designed to match the spaces on the gameboard, a large box of bingo chips

Players: 3-D Bingo is a game for up to eight players or up to eight teams with three or four players on each team.

Objective: The winning player or team is the first to fill the nine spaces on the gameboard. Correct answers allow spaces to be covered with bingo chips.

How to Play: Players must cover all nine spaces on the gameboard. Members of a team are encouraged to help one another search for correct answers. The teacher or game leader is to explain to the players that bingo chips may only be placed on a space if *both the answer and color are correct*. The teacher will be using the set of calling cards that are provided for these eight gameboards. When using the calling card, it is important that the leader *call the color first, then read the problem*!

Example:

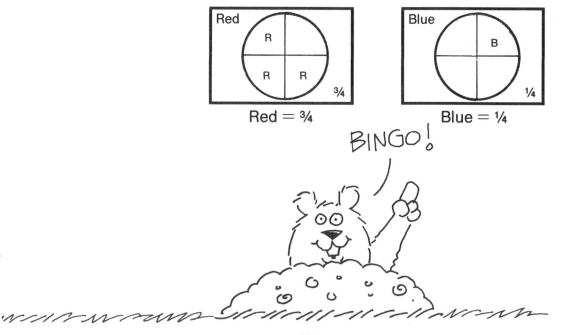

Red = ¾   Blue = ¼

BINGO!

GA1336

After the teacher calls the color and reads the fraction, the teacher is to show the calling card to the players.

The calling cards and the gameboards should be photocopied. Use magic markers to color in the fractional parts on the calling cards and the gameboards.

The color code is R = red, B = blue, Y = yellow, O = orange. Use soft shades when possible.

Here are some additional examples of 3-D gameboards. Remember that with each example you will need up to eight gameboards as well as calling cards.

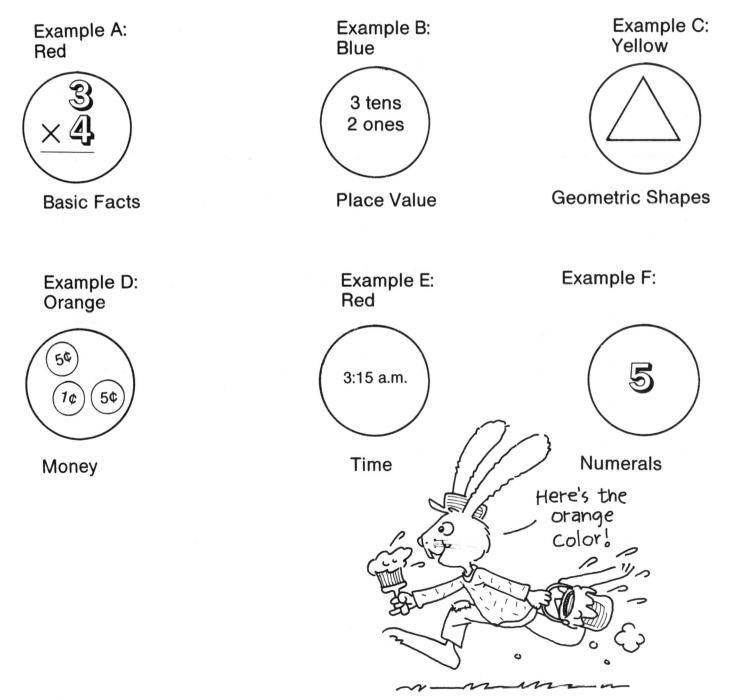

Example A:
Red

$$3 \times 4$$

Basic Facts

Example B:
Blue

3 tens
2 ones

Place Value

Example C:
Yellow

Geometric Shapes

Example D:
Orange

5¢
1¢ 5¢

Money

Example E:
Red

3:15 a.m.

Time

Example F:

5

Numerals

Here's the orange color!

GA1336

Calling Cards for Fraction 3-D Bingo

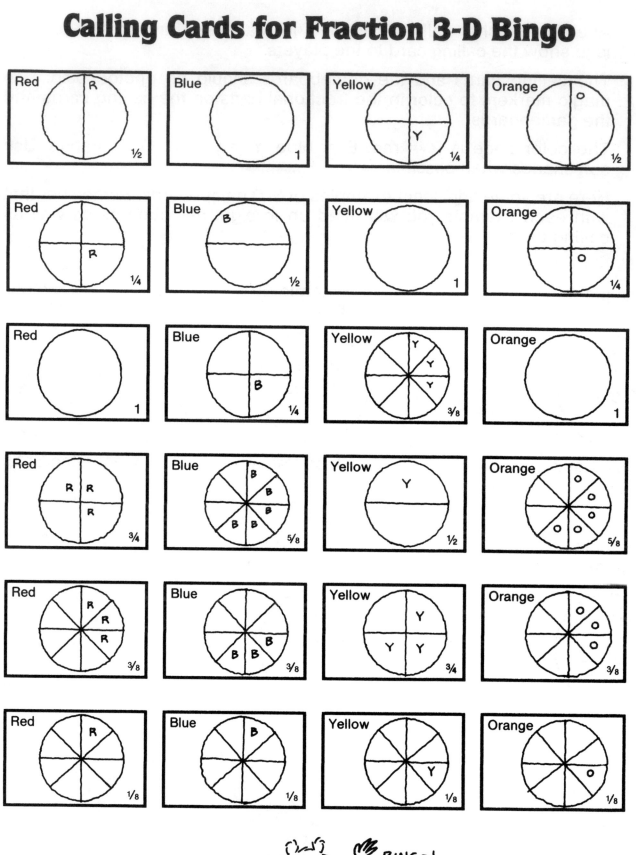

90

Gameboard Card A

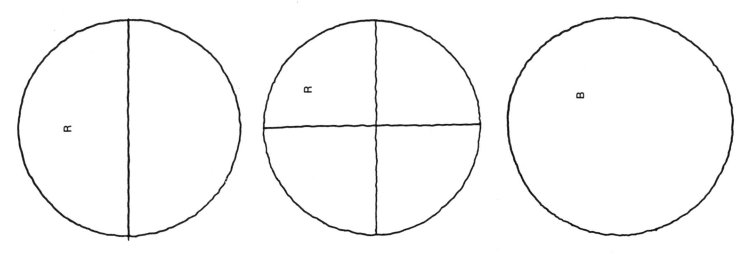

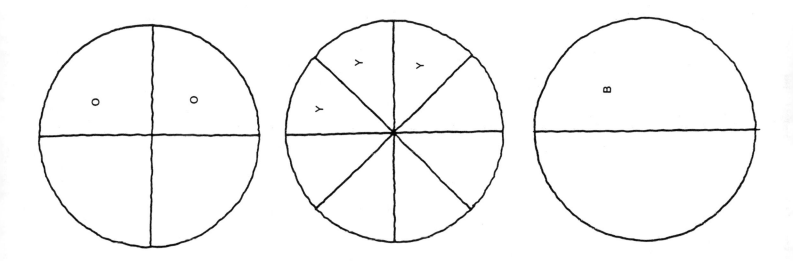

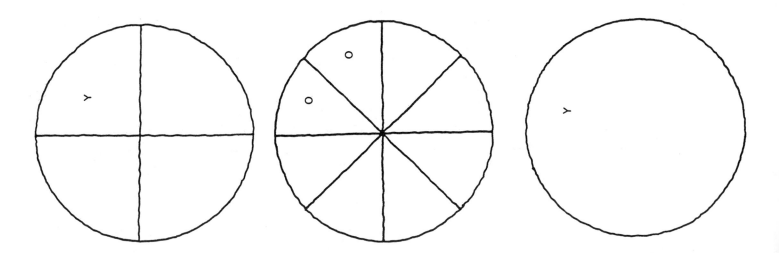

91

Gameboard Card B

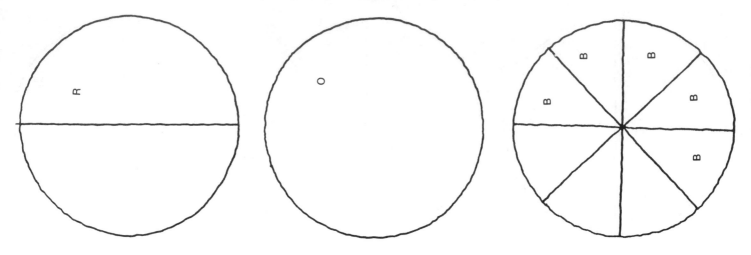

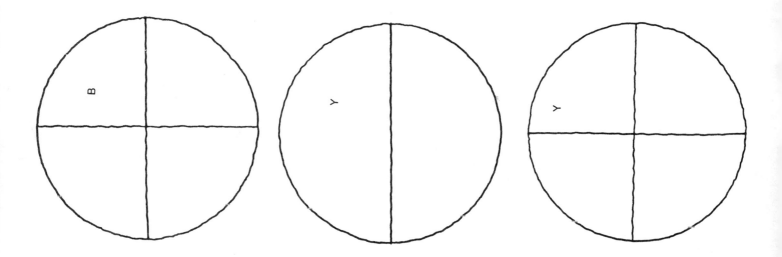

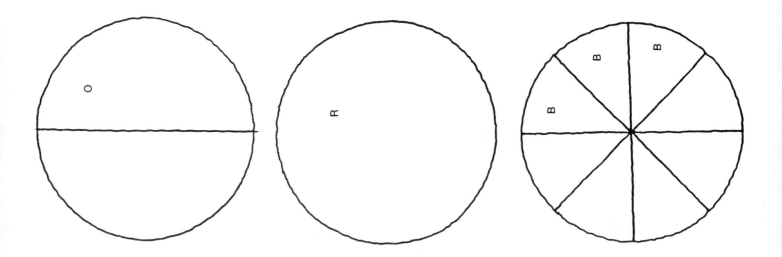

92

GA1336

Gameboard Card C

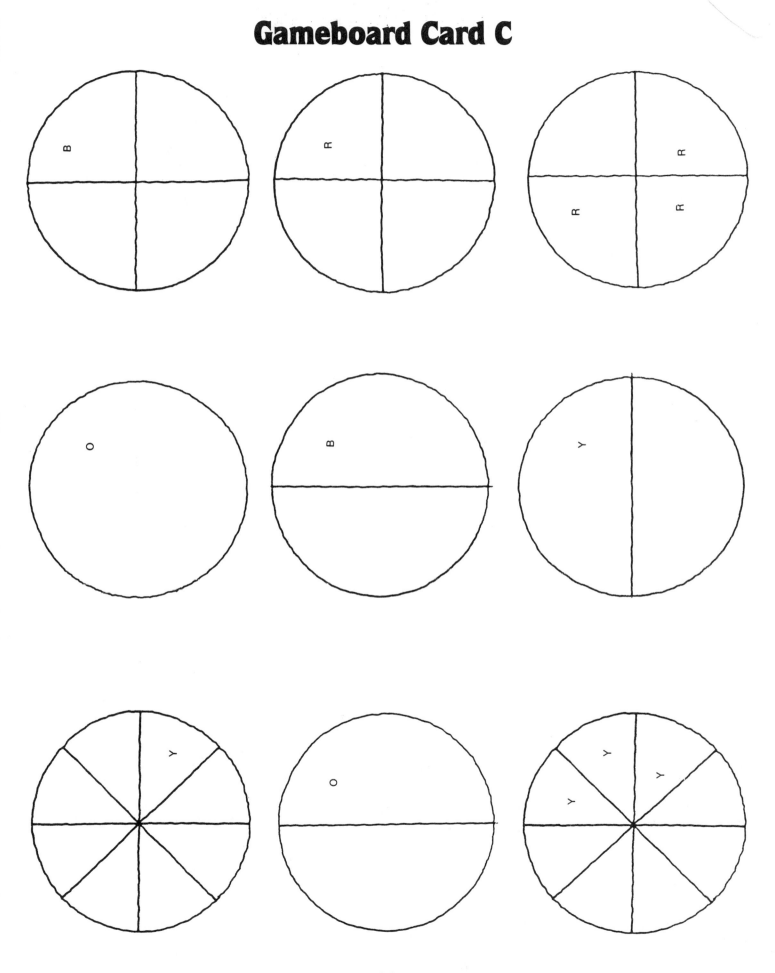

GA1336

Gameboard Card D

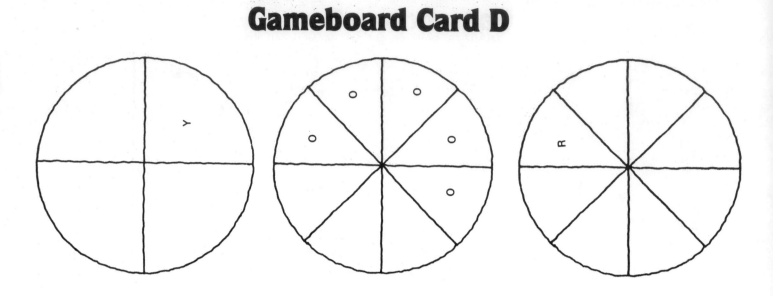

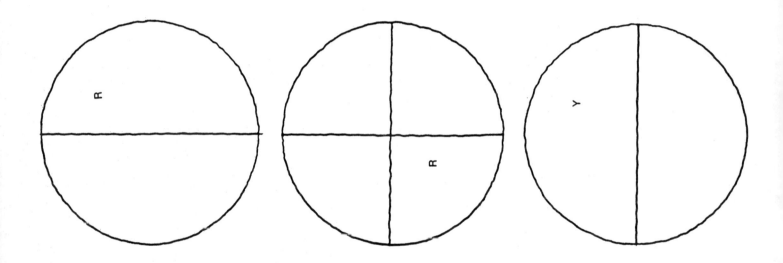

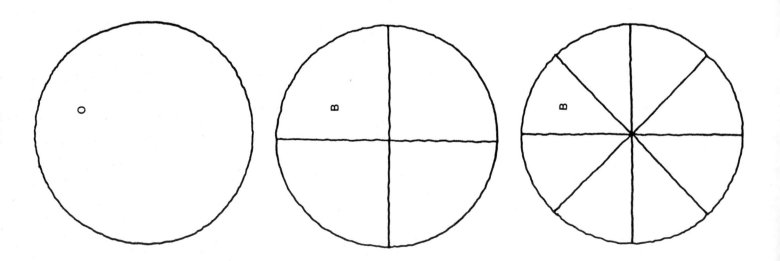

94

GA1336

Gameboard Card E

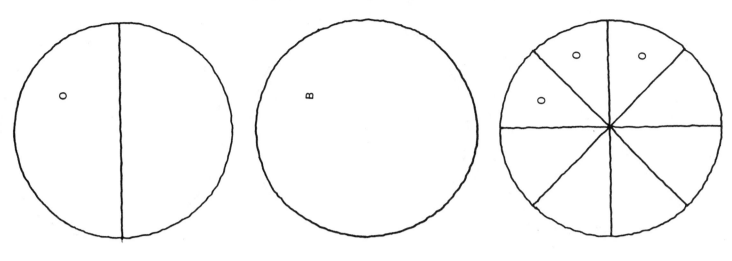

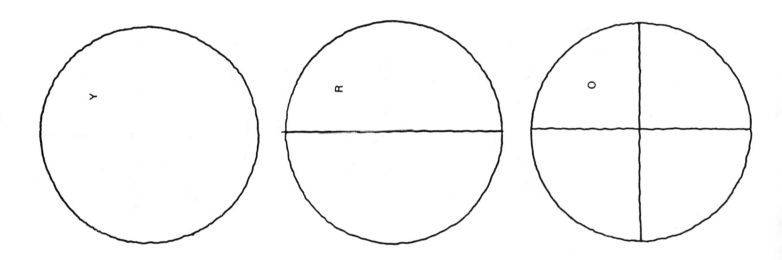

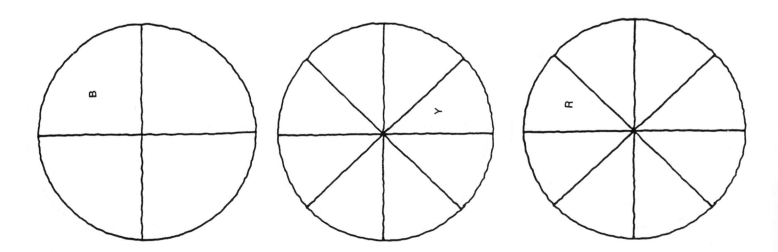

95

GA1336

Gameboard Card F

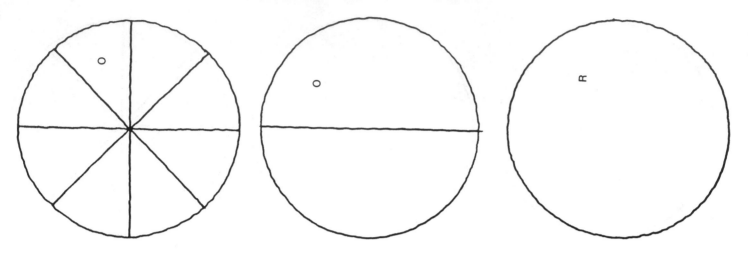

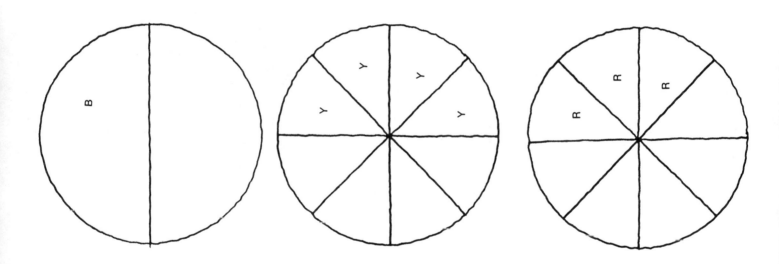

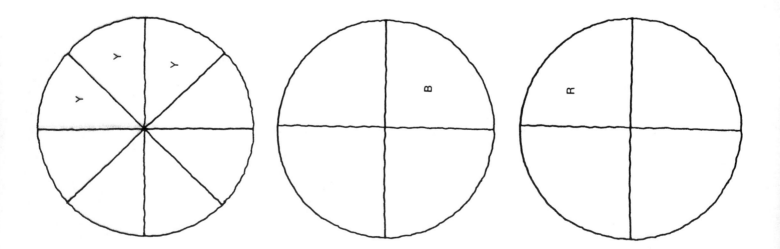

Gameboard Card G

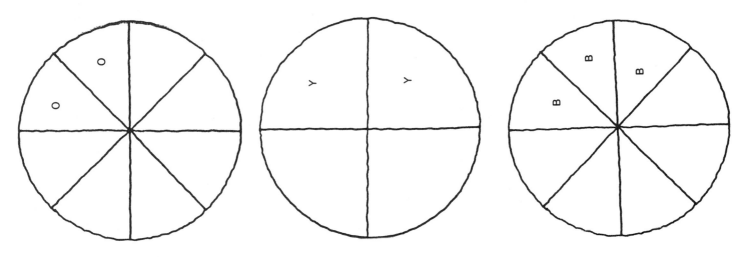

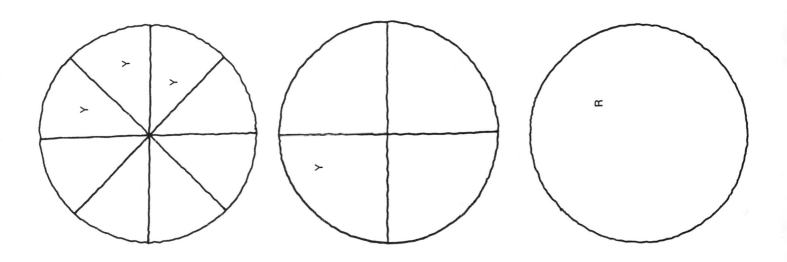

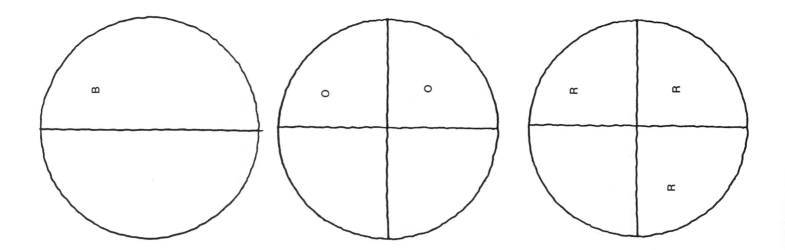

Gameboard Card H

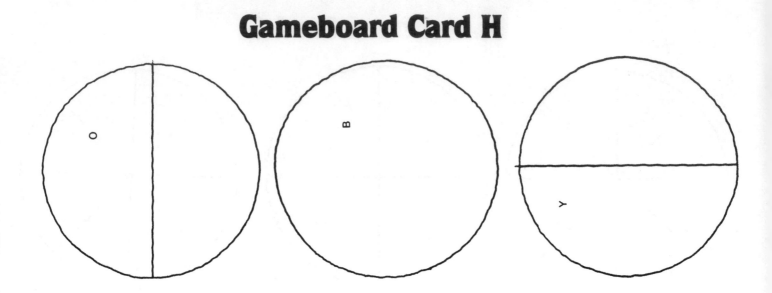

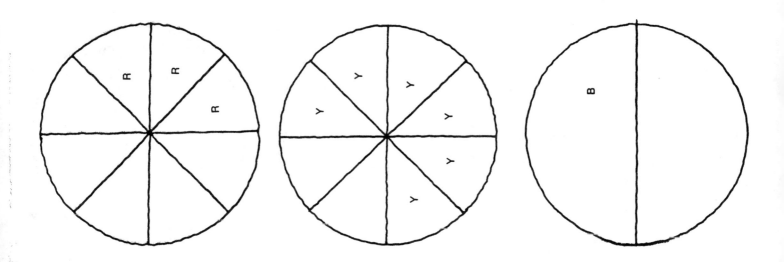

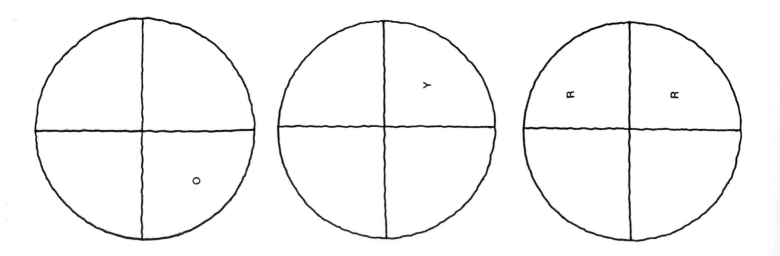

98

GA1336

Intermediate Chain

SKILLS: Basic Math Facts

The chain activity format is one that encourages excitement, enthusiasm and extremely high motivation. This is a drill that can be used with the entire class or by someone working alone. This particular chain is comprised of twenty links. Each link represents a specific math fact. Distribute these links to the class members. The starting point of the chain can be at any link. The student holding the initial link card is to read this card aloud and wait for the next student to read the only card that will correctly follow in a proper progression.

After reading his/her card, each student should pause and wait for the next player to read the appropriate card. Continue with this format until all of the cards have been read. The chain will be completed when the initial student is ready to read his/her card for the second time.

Once the class gets into the flow of the activity, you may want to introduce another dimension to the chain. This time you might want to use a stopwatch to determine how quickly the class was able to successfully complete the chain. Record this time and challenge the students. The challenge is to get a lower score each time the chain is attempted.

Front	Back	Front	Back
-1	I have negative 1. Who has negative 4 more?	1/4	I have 1/4. Who has 1/2 of it?
-5	I have negative 5. Who has plus 5 more?	1/8	I have 1/8. Who has 6/8 more?
0	I have zero. Who has 1 to the 5th power?	7/8	I have 7/8. Who has 78?
1	I have 1. Who has 1/2 of it?	78	I have 78. Who has 78 hundredths?
1/2	I have 1/2. Who has 1/2 of it?	.78	I have 78 hundredths. Who has a prime number?

INTERMEDIATE CHAIN SIGN·UP

GA1336

Front	Back	Front	Back
17	I have the prime number. Who has a multiple of 15?	**12**	I have 12. Who has its triple?
45	I have 45. Who has a mixed number?	**36**	I have 36. Who has ½ of it?
5 1/3	I have 5 1/3. Who has an improper fraction?	**18**	I have 18. Who has the sum of its digits?
16/4	I have 16/4. Who has this number reduced?	**9**	I have 9. Who has its square?
4	I have 4. Who has the lowest common multiple for 4 and 3?	**81**	I have 81. Who has 82 less?

I have 16/4. Who has this number reduced?

GA1336

Multiplication Chain

Front	Back	Front	Back
25	I have 25. Who has 7 x 6?	**40**	I have 40. Who has 5 x 7?
42	I have 42. Who has 9 x 9?	**35**	I have 35. Who has 10 x 10?
81	I have 81. Who has 4 x 8?	**100**	I have 100. Who has 9 x 1?
32	I have 32. Who has 8 x 9?	**9**	I have 9. Who has 7 x 3?
72	I have 72. Who has 9 x 7?	**21**	I have 21. Who has 6 x 5?
63	I have 63. Who has 10 x 4?	**30**	I have 30. Who has 5 x 5?

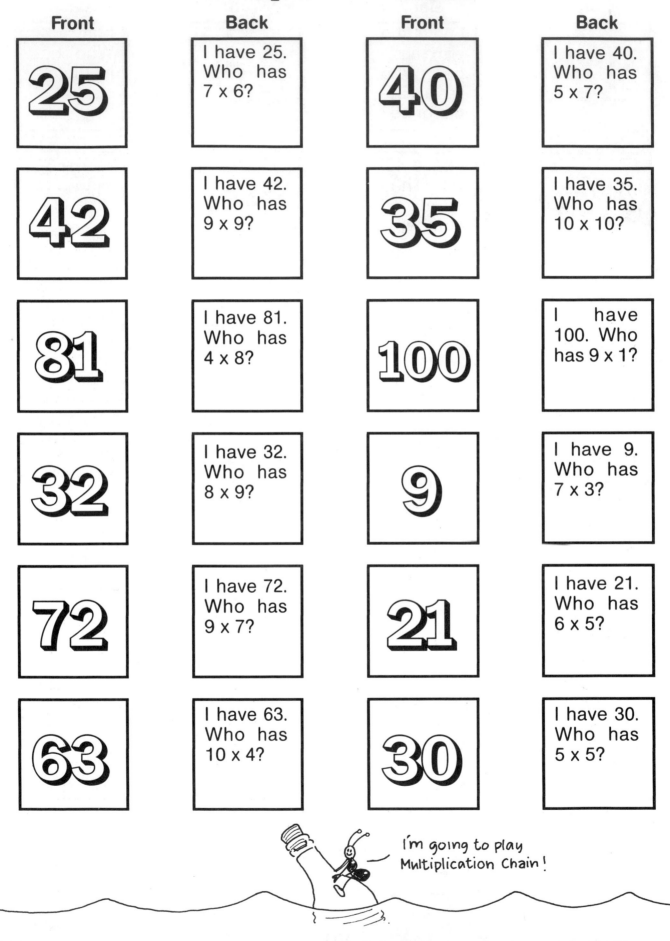

I'm going to play Multiplication Chain!

GA1336

Addition and Subtraction Primary Chain

Front	Back	Front	Back
2	I have 2. Who has 1 more?	**10**	I have 10. Who has 4 less?
3	I have 3. Who has 6 more?	**6**	I have 6. Who has 10 more?
9	I have 9. Who has 4 more?	**16**	I have 16. Who has 1 less?
13	I have 13. Who has 10 more?	**15**	I have 15. Who has 10 less?
23	I have 23. Who has 7?	**5**	I have 5. Who has 3 more?
7	I have 7. Who has 3 more?	**8**	I have 8. Who has 6 less?

Addition and Subtraction
Primary Chain
←

103

GA1336

Answer Key

You Are an Absolutely Totally Awesome and Outstanding Student! Pages 2, 3

Problem A
1. 31 consonants
2. 22 vowels
3. 18 syllables
4. most often used letters are *a* and *t*
5. percentage of vowels = 42%
   percentage of consonants = 58%

Problem B
1. 47 consonants
2. 28 vowels
3. 22 syllables
4. most often used letter is *o*
5. percentage of vowels = 37%
   percentage of consonants = 63%

Just a Guess! Pages 4, 6, 7

Problem A = 164, Problem B = 245, Problem C = 190

Change for a Dollar Page 15

A. 2 quarters
   4 dimes
   10 pennies

B. 1 half dollar
   1 quarter
   4 nickels
   5 pennies

C. 1 quarter
   6 dimes
   3 nickels

D. 3 quarters
   2 dimes
   5 pennies

E. 1 quarter
   4 dimes
   4 nickels
   15 pennies

F. 4 dimes
   10 nickels
   10 pennies

G. 1 half dollar
   8 nickels
   10 pennies

H. 8 dimes
   4 nickels

Hmm. . m. m. . Older Than I Thought Pages 17, 18

Page 17
A. = 147
B. = 132
C. = 79
D. = 116
E. = 124
F. = 168
G. = 35
H. = 91
I. = 11
J. = 13

Page 18
A. = 13 years, 5 months
B. = 7 years, 5 months
C. = 11 years, 6 months
D. = 8 years, 1 month
E. = 10 years, 7 months
F. = 11 years, 8 months
G. = 8 years, 8 months
H. = 9 years, 10 months
I. = 5 years, 7 months
J. = 7 years, 7 months

GA1336

Who Sees What I See? Page 22

A. × 2
B. × 10
C. − 2
D. × 7
E. (3 ×) + 4
F. (3 ×) + 1
G. square the number
H. square the number minus one

Brainteaser XII Pages 40-42

1. fact or . . . factor
2. ma th . . . math
3. ope ration . . . operation
4. per cent . . . percent
5. pri me . . . prime
6. mult I ple . . . multiple
7. ze ro . . . zero
8. ad ded . . . added
9. re a son . . . reason
10. me Dian . . . median
11. ar Ray . . . array
12. t went y . . . twenty
13. later al . . . lateral
14. me tric . . . metric
15. ang le . . . angle
16. ch art . . . chart
17. cub e . . . cube
18. de crease . . . decrease
19. de gree . . . degree
20. dia Mond . . . diamond
21. dig it . . . digit
22. d is cover . . . discover
23. h eight . . . height
24. ax is . . . axis
25. tot al . . . total
26. Tess elate . . . tesselate
27. slop e . . . slope
28. p i . . . pi
29. in ch . . . inch
30. po int . . point

Any Way You Look at It! (Palindromic Dates) Pages 62, 63

Jan.	Feb.	Mar.	Apr.	May	June	July	Aug.	Sept.	Oct.	Nov.	Dec.
101	202	303	404	505	606	707	808	909	1001	1111	1221
111	212	313	414	515	616	717	818	919			
121	222	323	424	525	626	727	828	929			
131											

Palindromic dates in a year—31

The numbers that represent all of the nonpalindromic dates can eventually be recorded as a palindrome.

Example: February 16 216
reverse the digits;
then add 612
_____
828

June 5 605
reverse the digits;
then add 506
_____
1111

Some dates may take more steps when trying to reach the palindrome

Example: July 19 719
reverse the digits;
then add 917
_____
1636

reverse the digits;
then add 6361
_____
7997

Page 63

September 18
918
819
1737
7371
9108
8019
17127
72171
89298

August 26
826
628
1454
4541
5995

November 15
1115
5111
6226

March 29
329
923
1252
2521
3773

August 29
829
928
1757
7571
9328
8239
17567
76571
94138
83149
177287
782771
960058
850069
1810127
7210181
9020308
8030209
17050517
71505071
88555588

The Awesome Power of 2 Page 68

1st hour = 1 Time Blox
2nd hour = 2 Time Blox
3rd hour = 4 Time Blox
4th hour = 8 Time Blox
5th hour = 16 Time Blox
6th hour = 32 Time Blox
7th hour = 64 Time Blox
8th hour = 128 Time Blox
9th hour = 256 Time Blox
10th hour = 512 Time Blox
11th hour = 1024 Time Blox
12th hour = 2048 Time Blox
13th hour = 4096 Time Blox
14th hour = 8192 Time Blox
15th hour = 16,384 Time Blox
16th hour = 32, 768 Time Blox
17th hour = 65,536 Time Blox
18th hour = 131,072 Time Blox
19th hour = 262,144 Time Blox
20th hour = 524,288 Time Blox
21st hour = 1,048,576 Time Blox
22nd hour = 2,097,152 Time Blox
23rd hour = 4,194,304 Time Blox
24th hour = 8,388,608 Time Blox

*32,768 sheets of 8" x 10" paper

Close to 39! Page 69

Start

```
3 →1   9   5   2   6

2   0   8→4   1   3

5   7   8   2   0   1

4   2   3   5→7   9

6   1   2   5   3   3

8   5   9   4   2   6
```

$3 + 1 + 8 + 4 + 8 + 5 + 7 + 3 = 39$
7 moves

```
3   1   9   5→2   6

2   0   8←4   1   3

5   7   8   2   0   1

4   2   3←5   7   9

6   1   2   5   3   3

8   5   9   4   2   6
```
Start

$6 + 3 + 5 + 3 + 2 + 4 + 8 + 5 + 2 + 1 = 39$

Color Math with Food Page 84

A. 19 points = corn and butter topped with cherries
B. 7 points = orange slices and spinach on white bread
C. 14 points = blueberries and pickles scrambled in an egg
D. 21 points = red beets and green apples chopped and mixed with milk
E. 18 points = cherries with mustard
F. 20 points = watermelon with asparagus

GA1336